P9-DOG-321

Thunder from the Mountain

John A. Stroman

THUNDER FROM THE MOUNTAIN

The Ten Commandments Today

UPPER ROOM BOOKS

N ASHVILLE

Thunder from the Mountain

Copyright © 1990 by John A. Stroman. All rights reserved.

No part of this book may be reproduced in any manner whatsoever without written permission of the publisher except in brief quotations embodied in critical articles or reviews. For information address The Upper Room, 1908 Grand Avenue, P.O. Box 189, Nashville, TN 37202.

Scripture quotations not otherwise identified are from the Revised Standard Version of the Bible, copyright 1946, 1952, and © 1971 by the Division of Christian Education, National Council of Churches of Christ in the USA, and are used by permission.

Scripture quotations designated TEV are from the *Good News Bible* - Old Testament: Copyright © American Bible Society 1976; New Testament: Copyright © American Bible Society 1966, 1971, 1976.

Scripture quotations designated REB are from the Revised English Bible, © Oxford University Press and Cambridge University Press 1989, and are used by permission of Cambridge University Press.

Excerpt from *Markings* by Dag Hammarskjöld, translated by Leif Sjöberg and W. H. Auden. Translation copyright © 1964 by Alfred A. Knopf, Inc. and Faber and Faber, Ltd. Reprinted by permission of the publishers.

"See the Super Patriot" © 1969 by E. C. Publications. Published in *The MAD Morality or The Ten Commandments Revisited* by Vernard Eller. Copyright © 1970 by Abingdon Press. Reprinted by permission of E. C. Publications, Inc.

To Viv

In appreciation for all of her love and support

Contents

PREFACE

The Ten Commandments are helpful to us in comprehending our mission and ministry in a global context. These chapters on the commandments are the result of months of study together as pastor and people at Pasadena Community Church in St. Petersburg, Florida, where I serve as the senior pastor.

I have sought to approach this series with serious theological and textual inquiry without, I hope, becoming overly pedantic. I have tried to follow the trajectory of each commandment as it moves from the text to contemporary moral, ethical, and theological implications. In the "Introduction" I have dealt with some important issues that I feel every preacher, teacher, or other inquiring believer needs to keep in mind as he or she approaches the Ten Commandments. At the end is a list of questions and comments for further consideration and discussion along with a listing of suggested resources for additional study.

I hope that this volume will increase our knowledge of the Old Testament, adding to its richness for both preaching and teaching while bringing to light some of its latent wealth for Christian living.

I am indebted to many people who have been a source

of encouragement and inspiration for this study. I am grateful to the members of my parish; their response and feedback have added immeasurably to these chapters.

I want to express a special thanks to Patrick D. Miller, Jr., professor of Old Testament studies at Princeton Theological Seminary, for his comments and insight. I sincerely appreciate my colleagues Jim Harnish and Dan Johnson, who read this material critically. Above all, I want to express my deepest appreciation to Vivian, my wife, whose love, support, and enthusiasm have made this volume possible.

INTRODUCTION

The Ten Commandments for today's world are vital and irreplaceable. They provide for our modern world basic, concrete, and fundamental guidelines for living. Here is a set of principles we can teach our children that are absolutely right and binding for a lifetime.

The moral climate of our communities has changed dramatically. I was amazed when a national news report revealed that in 1940, public school administrators listed the most outstanding problems among the student body as chewing gum, talking out in class, running in the halls, and loitering. Today, the list includes drug and alcohol abuse, teenage pregnancy, rape, and assaults on teachers. Today's moral and ethical confusion has resulted from the fracturing of the family, confusion over human sexuality, crime in such high places as the federal government, and loss of credibility in certain segments of the religious television empire. In the morass of this moral and ethical confusion the commandments are indispensable to us. They define for us what human liberty is, what freedom of the spirit means; they deepen our understanding of morality in both our personal and corporate lives.

The commandments are so practical, so real to life. Those who discover God and make God the primary center of life and living seem to have a focal point, a center of reality, that enables them to integrate all other aspects of living. Out of the mystery of this relationship comes a respect for other men and women as well as a sense of harmony with all God's creation.

The commandments are functional in human life. Those who refrain from stealing, committing adultery, killing, and taking unfair advantage of others find life far more satisfying than those who practice such behavior. People who have time for reflection, rest, and worship seem to cope with life better than those who do not. Those who respect the laws of creation seem to get more from life as they cooperate with nature rather than resisting or abusing it. The fourth commandment—"Remember the sabbath day, to keep it holy"—has a great deal to say about this.

Possibly the most valuable aspect of the Ten Commandments is their practical application in regard to our corporate and social life together. One of the primary functions of the Ten Commandments is to provide the adhesiveness necessary to form the community of God's people. For Jews or for Christians who are seeking to live in community, the Ten Commandments are essential.

THE DECALOGUE

In Hebrew the Ten Commandments are called "the ten words" (the Decalogue), the ten unchanging words of God spoken directly to the people (Deut. 5:4). The Decalogue appears in two locations in the Old Testament, in Exodus 20 and in Deuteronomy 5.

The two accounts are prompted by two different historical settings. The account in Exodus 20 tells of the Decalogue's initial transmission to Israel, whereas in Deuteronomy 5 Moses restates the Decalogue to the people prior to their entering the promised land. Here Moses is reminding the people that these words comprise the basic character for their life together in the land that the Lord is giving to them.

The Decalogue is almost identical in the two accounts. A difference can be seen in the form of the fourth commandment (Ex. 20:8-11; Deut. 5:12-15), a difference reflective of the distinction between the early wilderness experience and the end of the Hebrews' wanderings. For the most part, I will refer to the commandments as they appear in Exodus 20.

In both the Exodus and the Deuteronomy accounts, the Decalogue is located at the starting point of the legal material and occupies a primary place in divine instruction. This placement gives significant clues that these words are special. Patrick Miller points out that all of the law is God-given, but the story singles out the Decalogue as having special importance, lifting it to a higher level than the rest of the law.

Because the social and economic situations of community are forever changing, the immediate significance of the Decalogue may change from time to time and from environment to environment, but the foundation does not change. These "ten words" given by God remain forever the same. They provide the foundation essential for maintaining community, the principles necessary for the design of modern life in today's world.

GRACE BEFORE THE LAW

In the Exodus-event, Israel experienced God's grace powerfully and dramatically. Chronologically, then, deliverance preceded the Decalogue. The "gospel" of deliverance is placed at the head of the law. During the Exodus Israel encountered a God of liberation and freedom. In "the drama of the brickyard," according to Walter Brueggemann, Israel's theology crystallized out of experience.

In Exodus 3:7-8, the verbs are important because they express the character of God's nature in relationship to Israel prior to the giving of the Ten Commandments at Sinai. God *saw* the affliction of the people, *heard* their cry of pain and oppression, *knew* their suffering, and *came down* and *delivered* them out of their bondage. Therefore, God is described as the God "who brought you out of the land of Egypt, out of the house of bondage" (Exod. 20:2). This experience of grace resulting in freedom never ceases to inspire and give direction to Israel's faith. All the events of that history not only revealed God to the people but also redeemed them through God's love. The remembrance of this mighty act of grace was essential for the continuation of the Exodus experience.

Trust and confidence in God resulted from Israel's experience of the Exodus. From that factual moment when God's hand was upon these freed slaves, they thought backwards and forwards, upwards and outwards, drawing firm conclusions about the purpose, origin, and destiny of the world under God.

The Exodus event united the people in a community. This experience was indelibly etched on their minds and hearts and eventually shaped the liturgy, celebration, and the very life of the community. The Israelite people accepted the obligation of both covenant and community in gratitude for what God had already done on their behalf. From the beginning, divine grace and divine demand, gospel and law, were inseparably connected in Israel's experience.

The point is this: The saving act of God in human history, which produced the saved community, becomes the saving message that the community is to preserve and proclaim. At the very beginning of the Ten Commandments (Exod. 20:2), this saving act is recognized and therefore the commandments begin with the self-disclosure of the love of God. Hope and grace stand at the threshold to the commandments. The community's experience of grace as expressed in liberation, deliverance, and freedom is the context in which the "oughts" of the Decalogue are both expressed and observed.

Brueggemann points out in *Living Toward a Vision* that "Sinai is a probing of what the exodus means. . . . Sinai is specific and demanding, but its claim and its power are of the exodus variety. . . . The 'oughts' of Sinai have no claim on those who do not remember being awakened in the night of fear and freedom to dance in the morning on the other side of the water. . . . biblical morality is in a story rather than a set of rules."

The words in Exodus 20:2 are important to remember: "I am the Lord your God, who brought you out of the land of Egypt, out of the house of bondage." This is a proclamation of triumph *for* God's people, not over them. What follows is an expression of *grace*, not of compulsion. This means that to omit verse two in a recitation of the Ten Commandments is to put them in a false setting, in one of law rather than of grace.

TORAH

Torah is the Old Testament term for divine instruction and guidance, particularly through the law. Torah is much more teaching and instruction than it is law. The Torah is not simply legislation. It is all that God has made known of God's nature, character, and purpose, and what God would have men and women be and do.

The term *Torah* seems to have gone through several shifts in meaning:

(1) In early passages, priestly instruction is provided on the basis of oracles and traditional understanding of the requirements of God.

(2) Later *Torah* refers to the basic instruction provided to Israel by God, especially in regard to legal matters.

(3) By the time of Ezra *Torah* meant the substance of the Pentateuch, the books of Moses.

(4) Finally, *Torah* becomes the standard term for the Pentateuch in its entirety, as distinguished from the Prophets and the other books.

According to Walter Brueggemann in *Hope in History*, for Israel the Torah was essential because the liberation of Israel in Egypt is not only a *"liturgic* act (The Song of Moses) [in Deuteronomy 32] or a *political* act (of changing sovereigns of Sinai). It is also a *legislative* act. . . . It may begin in dreams, but it leads to acts of public shaping derived from the dreams. Israel could begin by a new and joyous dance, but then it had to translate the power and intention of the dance into economic and political terms. This is the work of torah."

The word *torah* is often associated with the word *halak,* "to walk" (Exod. 16:4; Isa. 2:3; Jer. 9:13; Ps. 119:1). It is used in these instances as an instruction given to a person for the purpose of walking on a straight path. It is a word that expresses God's will for the way we are to journey (Exod. 4:12-15). The basic root of *torah* is the Hebrew word *yara.* It literally means "to throw" or "to cast." Earl F. Palmer makes this observation in *Old Law—New Life*: "A teacher, a *moreh,* points toward the way accurately, so that the teacher's pupil is able to find the place where the way leads. The *moreh* throws the rock clearly and straight ahead; so in a similar fashion the law shows the way." This all seems to suggest that *torah* is to be a daily guide in the life of the people (Ps. 25:8-12).

16

Biblical scholars surmise that the Ten Commandments were put in their present form during the period of the Exile (587–538 BCE). The commandments have been divided into two sections: the first through the fourth, concerning religious duties; the fifth through the tenth, concerning moral duties. In other words, the first section deals with our personal relationship with God, and the second section our relationships with one another. Earl F. Palmer takes this one step further and expresses the Ten Commandments in terms of four relationships:

(1) The relationship of a human being toward God is the first relationship portrayed in the Ten Commandments. The first three commandments describe that relationship.
(2) The second is the relationship with ourselves, which is implied throughout the commandments but is in primary focus in the fourth and fifth commandments.
(3) The next relationship, toward the neighbor, is the primary focus of the fifth through tenth commandments.
(4) The fourth relationship might be described as our relationship toward the earth, the whole of the created order. Each of the commandments contains implications that come together and provide a Torah perspective with regard to this relationship.

These four relationships together define a human being, according to Palmer. "When any one of the four relationships is in confusion or distortion, that crisis of brokenness will gravely affect the other parts of the whole." Within the Ten Commandments we can discover both God's grand design and our place within it.

THUNDER FROM THE MOUNTAIN

Thunder, lightning, fire, and smoke surrounded the giving of the law. The experience at Sinai was one that the Hebrews were not to forget. As the people stood at the foot

17

of the mountain, the mountain itself glowed with the light of fire, its brightness contrasted sharply with the surrounding "darkness, cloud, dense mist." Through the thunder on the mountain, Israel sensed the presence of God. There was no physical representation or form but only God's voice.

In pagan religions the violent acts of nature and the turbulent atmospheric disturbances are taken literally to be the very lives of the gods themselves. But not so in the scriptures; here fire, wind, thunder, and smoke are not God but simple, powerful, poetic forms that represent the consciousness of the intensified presence of God at a particular moment in time. The description of Elijah's experience in this same wilderness of Horeb illustrates this distinction:

> *And behold, the Lord passed by, and a great and strong wind rent the mountains, and broke in pieces the rocks before the Lord, but the Lord was not in the wind; and after the wind an earthquake, but the Lord was not in the earthquake; and after the earthquake a fire, but the Lord was not in the fire; and after the fire a still small voice.*
> *1 Kings 19:11-12*

These elaborate descriptions of the upheavals of nature communicate something of the ultimately inexpressible, mysterious manifestations of the Divine Presence among the people. We must remember above all, with Elijah as well as with Moses, that God is revealed through God's *word*. The *word* reaches its ultimate expression in John 1:14, "And the Word became flesh and dwelt among us, full of grace and truth."

LAW IN THE NEW TESTAMENT

Any serious discussion of the Ten Commandments must consider the place of the law in the New Testament.

There is no evidence that Jesus at any time repudiated the Ten Commandments. He made his view clear: "Think not that I have come to abolish the law" (Matt. 5:17). He went on to say, "Not an iota, not a dot, will pass from the law until all is accomplished (Matt. 5:18). Jesus stressed that the law is so important that not the smallest detail of it will pass away. He startled his hearers by saying, "It has been said . . . but I say to you." He never once denied the validity of the commandments; rather, he made them immensely more demanding by going beyond the law of actions to one's inner thoughts and intents.

Notice the similarity between the Sermon on the Mount and Jesus on the one hand, and the law on Mount Sinai and Moses on the other. The writer of Matthew intends us to see this affinity. On Mount Sinai Moses delivers the law of the earlier covenant to Israel. In the Sermon on the Mount, Matthew portrays Jesus as the new Moses giving a new law to a new Israel as the people of God. For Matthew this event marked the coming together of the old and the new. The old was not being denied or replaced; rather, it was being enriched and enhanced. Both the old and the new deal with human life and living. For Israel this was the right word at the right time. God, after the Exodus, sought to bring the people into community. God gave the law to Moses as a means of binding their hearts together.

The New Testament has no intention of abolishing the law. Paul states that "Christ is the end of the law" (Rom. 10:4). The word Paul uses for *end* is *telos*, which does not mean the final cessation of something. Rather, *telos* means the *accomplishment* of the purpose for which something was originally designed. The goal of the law—a right relationship with God—is accomplished at last in Jesus Christ.

Paul defines the law as the *schoolmaster* (in the King James Version), bringing us to Christ that we might be justified by faith (Gal. 3:24). The word used in the Revised

Standard Version is *custodian*. But neither word is completely accurate. The word in question here is *paidagogos*, meaning a slave whose duty it was to take a boy to school, deliver him to the schoolmaster, and take him home after school. The *paidagogos* did not go to school himself, but merely handed the boy over to the teacher.

How does this concept relate to the law? For Paul, the law drove him to despair, so that in the end he gave up the impossible task of trying to save himself and threw himself into the arms of a merciful God. For Paul the law is like the *paidagogos*, leading him to the school of Christ and leaving him there. So the failure of the law at this point might well be the beginning of the Christian faith for the believer.

THE DECALOGUE IN LITURGY

Frequent use of the Decalogue did not appear in Christian worship until the Reformation. After that time, the church used the Decalogue as part of its liturgical expression, in its preaching, and in its spiritual and moral witness to the community and the world, in both the Lutheran and the Reformed churches.

William Carl, in "The Decalogue in Liturgy, Preaching, and Life" (*Interpretation*, July 1989), contends that the twentieth century has seen a decline in the use of the Decalogue in worship. It is not present in the 1978 *Lutheran Book of Worship*, nor is it in the *1984 Supplemental Liturgical Resource I: The Service for The Lord's Day* of the Presbyterian Church USA, the *Directory of Worship* of the same church, or the 1989 *United Methodist Hymnal*. When Laurence Hull Stookey, who played an important role in the revision of *The Methodist Hymnal*, was questioned about the Decalogue's omission, he expressed surprise that it had been left out. Stookey believes that Lent would be an especially appropriate time to employ the Ten Commandments in worship, because of Lent's emphasis on both penitence and, in some denominations, instruction in the faith as preparation for Baptism or Confirmation.

Through revisions in the worship resources of mainline churches over the last decade, the use of the Decalogue, according to Carl, "has dropped out of sight liturgically, except among Episcopalians where its position is at best weakened." Why? Do we find its message too blunt, too offensive for our "live-and-let-live" society, too demanding of us? Some have suggested that churches do not want to offend people because many of the major denominations are already in decline, so we avoid the Decalogue. I agree with William Carl's response in this same article from *Interpretation*:

> People are not leaving our mainline churches because they have tried them and found them difficult but because they have tried them and found them too easy, too soft.
> The claims of Christ are not easy claims. Neither is the Decalogue. . . . In worship the Decalogue can point us in that right direction.

The Ten Commandments are irreplaceable as an instrument for moral value and teaching. They are essential not only for our individual life but also for our corporate and communal life together. The church's decision not to use them in corporate worship is a liturgical loss. It took the Reformation to make the Decalogue a vital part of our liturgical life; allowing the Decalogue to drift into disuse is a pity. Facing the moral ambiguity of today's permissive society, the church needs to bring the Decalogue fully into its liturgy and instruction in the faith.

The First Commandment

WHO IS NUMBER ONE?

You shall have no other gods before me (Exodus 20:3).

The competition to be number one is fierce. Each year millions of dollars are spent by Ford, GM, and Chrysler to be number one in the automotive world. TV executives do all in their power to inspire and motivate their writers, producers, and advertisers to be number one in the Nielsen ratings. Every movie producer hopes, labors, and dreams of capturing that one coveted award—the Oscar. For many that is the ultimate number one!

The first commandment makes a very candid, forthright statement, clear and unequivocal: "I am the Lord your God and you shall have no other gods before me." Without the slightest hesitation Moses declared that the God who brought Israel out of the land of Egypt and out of the house of bondage is number One!

What audacity! To say that God is the only God and we shall have no other gods. What is the basis for such exclusiveness? To many, it is an insult to their intelligence. There was a time when it may have appeared as a reasonable demand, a time when the gaps between the known and unknown were wide and mystery was a way of life, but not today. Thanks to science and technology many of the gaps have been narrowed, many problems have been solved or at least seem solvable, and many mysteries have been explained, pushing God to the perimeters of life. Hearing the words of this commandment today, we are not so much impressed by the concept of Yahweh as the only God as we are challenged about our belief in the existence of God at all.

It is difficult for us to imagine that we are claimed by a God who is our redeemer and deliverer, a God who will tolerate no rival. To give first place or even consideration to a God who demands fullest allegiance and declares that we are to have no other gods is an idea that can hardly be entertained seriously by secularized and sophisticated men and women of today's world.

However, it is convenient to know that God is out there—even if God is on the perimeter. You never know, someday we may face a colossal gap and we may need to dust God off and bring God back from the outer limits. We adhere to a kind of practical atheism, calling upon God only when we have a need; otherwise God is ignored as though nonexistent.

This kind of theology is more prevalent than one might think. For many people, their growing knowledge of the universe has made their childish thoughts of God inadequate. Instead of acquiring a worthier and larger idea of God to meet the needs and challenges of our modern world, they have given up all thoughts of a vital God whatsoever. This is expressed effectively by Sam Foss in the following poem:

> *A boy was born 'mid little things,*
> *Between a little world and sky,*
> *And dreamed not of the cosmic rings*
> *'Round which the circling planets fly.*

He lived in little works and thoughts,
Where little ventures grow and plod,
And paced and ploughed his little plots
And prayed unto his little God.

But, as the mighty system grew,
His faith grew faint with many scars;
The cosmos widened in his view,
But God was lost among his stars.

It is not so much that people do not believe in God but rather that God has been "lost among the stars." Other things have moved in and taken over and God is given a secondary place at best. God has lost number one status. Some people boldly declare by their demeanor that money, sex, and power are now number one. This attitude is flaunted vigorously by the media, from *People* magazine to the television program "Lifestyles of the Rich and Famous."

GOD'S GRACE COMES FIRST

In the absence of grace, this first commandment comes across as empty and hollow words, strange-sounding and making unreasonable demands for loyalty and devotion. Without knowledge of God's grace, the natural response to the demand of this commandment is, "So what?" It is difficult to have affection for this command of God if one has not experienced the grace of God.

But this command has antecedents; it has a history; it has flesh and blood on it that cannot be ignored. It is not abstract but rather has a context keenly expressed in Deuteronomy 7:6-9:

For you are a people holy to the Lord your God; the Lord your God has chosen you to be a people for his own possession, out of all the peoples that are on the face of the earth. It was not because you were more in number than any other people that the Lord set his love upon you and chose you, for you were the fewest of all peoples; but it is because the Lord loves you, and is keeping the oath which he swore to your fathers, that the Lord has brought you out with a mighty hand, and redeemed you from the house of bondage, from the hand of Pharaoh king of Egypt. Know therefore that the Lord your God is God, the faithful God who keeps covenant and steadfast love with those who love him and keep his commandments, to a thousand generations.

RECOGNIZING WHAT IS PRIMARY FOR US

In our consideration of this first commandment we need to ask ourselves, What significant word does it have for us today? First, we all have an absolute—that object or person in whom we place absolute trust. That absolute, whatever it is, ends up controlling and directing our lives. Think how tragically small and narrow life becomes when the center of that life is self, material wealth, position, power, sex, or drugs. However, many times our struggles are not between evil and good, but between good and a lesser good. We are constantly tempted to make secondary things primary. In the process we lose sight of what is essential, forcing us to live with second-best. That which is highest, most meaningful and fulfilling is forfeited by our willingness to be satisfied with mediocrity. How easy it is to make the wrong use of a good thing, merely for the sake of convenience or comfort. For instance, patriotism is a good thing but not when it becomes the only thing. Some time ago I came across this bit of verse in *The MAD Morality or The Ten Commandments Revisited*:

See the Super Patriot.
Hear him preach how he loves his country.
Hear him preach how he hates "Liberals" . . .
And "Moderates" . . . and "Intellectuals" . . .
And "Activists" . . . and "Pacifists" . . .
And "Minority Groups" . . . and "Aliens" . . .
And "Unions" . . . . and "Teenagers" . . .
And the "Very Rich" . . . and the "Very Poor"
And "People with Foreign–Sounding Names."
Now you know what a Super Patriot is.
He's someone who loves his country
While hating 93% of the people who live in it.

We are tempted to give primary importance to secondary issues, by placing someone or something that is less than God at the center of our lives. The result is that we become less than the persons God intended. When we give a mere fraction of ourselves to God, then we become a mere fraction of what we could be.

UNDERSTANDING THE NATURE OF GOD

Second, the chances are that we will become like the god we worship. What we believe influences who we are and what we do. For that very reason the Ten Commandments begin by insisting that there is one God, carefully defining God's nature and character, because theology and ethics are inseparable. Our theology is vitally important, because it is the basis of personal action. What we believe or do not believe about God has a profound effect on the way we treat others. From the very beginning it was necessary for Israel, as God's people, to understand correctly the nature of God, because this would deeply influence Israel's self-understanding and relationships with other people. How important this is for us—to understand who God is and what God has done. When we become aware of how God cares for us and relates to us, then we understand how we are to care for and relate to one another.

A strange and misguided theology supports strange and misguided actions. In our own times we have seen this powerfully demonstrated—from the Third Reich to Jonestown. To worship a licentious god like Baal can often produce a licentious person. A stern god produces a stern people as the world has so often tragically seen. A recent illustration of a misguided theology is the conduct of certain television preachers. Their bizarre behavior is the result of a theology that has gone astray—allowing money, wealth, and power to become the controlling factors in their ministry. These people have given primary importance to secondary issues.

It was essential for Israel to remember who this one God is. It was difficult to give reverence to the Greek gods with their loves and wars, their hates and adulteries, their cunning and trickery. No one can revere capricious, immoral, impure gods. Because God is in history, intricately involved with Israel's struggles and turmoils, the people saw firsthand God's justice, holiness, and love. Devotion, worship, and reverence was possible, not simply because God exists, but because of their personal knowledge of God. God is the God of Abraham, Isaac, and Jacob as well as of Sarah, Rebekah, and Rachel. God is just and loving, and it is essential that the chosen people be a just and loving people. The nature of this one eternal, almighty, just, and loving God deeply affects not only who they are, but what they will do.

The story is told that in 1939, as the Nazis were moving into the Netherlands, Henry Kramer, a Dutch theologian, was asked by a group of Christian lay people, "Our Jewish neighbors are disappearing from their homes. What must we do?" Kramer answered, "I cannot tell you what to do. I can tell you who you are. If you know who you are you will know what to do." These persons became part of the Dutch Resistance Movement. If we remember who our God is and that we are God's people, this will determine and define our conduct and personal relationships.

A CELEBRATION OF GOD'S OMNIPOTENCE

Unequivocally the Decalogue declares that God, who brought Israel from the tyranny of Pharaoh, is number One! God is a personal and loving God, who saw the affliction of the people, heard their cries of suffering and pain, and delivered them from the oppressive hand of their taskmasters.

God is the center of the universe, the sustainer of all beings, and the one upon whom Israel's entire life depends. The first commandment is the foundation of biblical religion as a whole. For Israel this commandment marks the radical rejection of polytheism and highlights the oneness of God. The *Shema*, "Hear, O Israel: The Lord our God is one Lord" (Deut. 6:4), serves as a forceful affirmation of faith.

It has been suggested that there is only one commandment, "You shall have no other gods before me," to which everything else is simply commentary. When this one God spoke there was no other to contradict; when God promised, there was no other to revoke that promise; when God warned, there was no other to provide refuge from that warning. In *The Book of Deuteronomy*, Peter C. Craigie asserts that God was more than the chief among a pantheon of gods (such as Baal in Canaan, Amon-Re in Egypt, or Marduk in Babylon). God was omnipotent, and God was the only God.

29

The first commandment begins in a very positive and dramatic fashion by its use of the intense personal pronoun—"No other gods before *me.*" The word for God is *Yahweh,* and it was first introduced to Moses at the time of the Exodus as the personal intransitive verb "I am." Now it becomes the name of God for Israel. In Hebrew the *name* means the *nature,* the *character,* the *personality,* of the person insofar as it is known or revealed. Those who know what God is like, who know God's nature and character, will put their trust in God. The importance of this name is not its linguistic value but its historical meaning. Yahweh is the God who is manifested as Israel's Redeemer, whose power humiliates Pharaoh, the highest ruler of the day, and who calls the forces of nature into service for historical purpose. The first verses of Exodus 20 clearly establish God as a personal God of character and concern. The only way to understand the Ten Commandments is to understand this innermost personal relationship between God and Israel. It was first and foremost an experience of love and grace. The Israelites were so overwhelmed that they celebrated the Exodus in song: "Who is like thee, O Lord, among the gods? . . . The Lord will reign for ever and ever" (Exod. 15:11, 18).

LIVING IN RELATIONSHIP TO THE ONE GOD

The implications and obligations of the first commandment are far-reaching in their significance. The command calls for a life-style dominated by one's relationship to God. For Israel, it affected the entire life of the whole covenant community. Its implications today remain the same. The relationship to this one God dominates every sphere of life, whether the life of action, thought, or emotion. There can be no area of life in which a person or object comes before the commitment to the one God. Anything that relegates the relationship with God to second place functions in effect as "another god." The demand of Jesus in regard to the gospel is, "Seek first his kingdom and his righteousness" (Matt. 6:33), and then let all other things find their proper place. The demand of the gospel has never been any less.

Who then is this God who demands such single-hearted devotion? Let me tell you! The only one and no other who is the ultimate Giver of all the good we have enjoyed. God is the Provider of life, health, home, and friends; the Source of the pleasures of prosperity, the blessings of adversity, the wonders of science, and the marvels of technology. God and no other is the supreme Disposer of the affairs of nations and the destinies of men and women; the Transformer who turns the wrath of men and women to his praises, humbles the proud and exalts the lowly.

God is the one who, in infinite, unfathomable love took human form in the person of Jesus Christ, born in Bethlehem and crucified on Calvary. In Christ, God became what we are that we might become what God is.

There is no other God in heaven, earth, or hell than the one who comes to us in Jesus of Nazareth, crucified, risen from the dead, and reigning eternally. It is God alone who gives us the commandment: "You shall have no other gods before me."

The Lord, God Almighty is number One—now and forevermore!

The Second Commandment

MAKING GOD IN OUR IMAGE

You shall not make for yourself a graven image, or any likeness of anything that is in heaven above, or that is in the earth beneath, or that is in the water under the earth; you shall not bow down to them or serve them; for I the Lord your God am a jealous God, visiting the iniquity of the fathers upon the children to the third and the fourth generation of those who hate me, but showing steadfast love to thousands of those who love me and keep my commandments (Exodus 20:4-6).

Why was Moses so upset when he returned from the mountaintop to find the people worshiping a golden bull (Exod. 32)? Wasn't God a bit narrow-minded to have given this second commandment? In making the idol of gold, the Israelites were merely following the universal instincts of humankind. What was wrong with a visible, tangible god like those of other nations? Certainly they had good motives—"We wanted a god to lead us." How comforting, especially in moments of travail and trial to point to an object and say, "There is God." How reassuring for the Israelites to locate and define God. Also, if God were fixed and located, God could be controlled and used for their own purposes and convenience. What's wrong with that? In making this idol they were merely trying to make God useful and practical.

The fact is the Israelites were literally in a tight spot. Wandering in the Wilderness of Sinai, they longed for leadership and direction, for something to trust, someone to follow. For certain, they could not return to Egypt and they had not yet seen the promised land. They were boxed in with the desert on one side and hostile enemies on the other. They besieged Aaron, "Give us a god. Everyone has a god." Aaron replied, "You have one. This is the God who brought you from Egypt." "What is this god like?" they replied. "This god doesn't even have a name. Moses calls God 'I AM.' What kind of name is that? Moses never describes God. In fact, he said he has only seen this god's back. What is our god like? God must have a name, a face, a shape. We must be able to bring our god offerings, sacrifices, carry our god into battle, show our god off to others, describe this god to our children. Give us a god!"

What on earth was Aaron to do? He did the best he could. Taking their gold bracelets, earrings, and jewelry he formed the universal symbol of strength and fertility—the bull. Aaron's acquiescence produced what the people wanted. There are advantages to making god in one's own image. Now their god was capable of being located, defined, seen, and above all controlled. When Aaron was challenged, he gave the weakest of explanations: "I threw the ornaments into the fire and out came the bull!"

Why was God so angry? Surely God could have been more understanding, especially after taking into consideration Israel's precarious situation. We need to consider the reasons that lie behind this great prohibition in the second commandment. We need to understand what this meant for Moses and the Israelite community.

WHAT CAN REPRESENT GOD?

Moses made a remarkable discovery about God at the
burning bush. It was in this encounter with God that the
liberator became liberated. Moses experienced God as the
"incomparable one," the "unrepresentable one," and
realized that no object or material in the created order
could remotely come close to depicting God. Moses said
even if one were to search the entire created order, heaven
above, earth beneath, or the water under the earth, there
is nothing in all of creation sufficient to portray God.

In straightforward terms the second commandment
places limitations upon Israel's worship: Do not set up a
graven image that would seek to represent God in your
worship site, your village, or your home. In the
experience of Sinai, when the people stood at the foot of
the mountain, there was a display of fire, thunder, and
lightning. It was a moment the Hebrews will never forget.
In this most profound, moving encounter with their God,
related in Deuteronomy 4:12, there was no physical
representation, no form of God, but only God's
voice—God's word. Any attempt to represent God in a
form would have been totally inadequate and misleading.

If no material in the entire created order suffices to
represent God, then who does represent God in the world
and among the nations? The only possible representation
of the living God is the living human being bearing the
image and breath of God, dedicated to doing God's will on
earth. Thus, as Walter Harrelson writes in *The Ten
Commandments and Human Rights*, "Israel is to *make* no
image of Yahweh, but Israel is to *be* an image of God in
the world. . . . When the people of Israel are faithful to
the God of the covenant, then God has the right kind of
representative in the world of humankind." Patrick Miller
has commented, "The only true image of God we have is
the one who walks on two feet."

Our greatest temptation today is to be less than adequate representatives of God's will and purpose for our lives. We transgress the second commandment mostly by what we fail to do rather than by what we do. It is in our failure to recognize God's image and purpose in ourselves and our inability to live out this divine call and purpose before the people of the world that we violate the commandment. To live for any purpose other than the will of God is idolatry. The commandment challenges us to consider several factors about the objects of our personal devotion.

THE SHALLOWNESS OF IDOLS

First, idols are static. They are stationary, devoid of meaning, feeling, and life. Isaiah (in chapter 44) looks with distress at the confusion caused among the people when they have turned their lives over to that which is false and empty. He cannot understand how human beings can give attention, devotion, and meaning to objects that have no power or feeling.

Isaiah found this strange indeed. He attacks idolatry with a bitter sarcasm and a stinging satire. He ridicules the idol and has some very scornful remarks for persons who make and worship them. You can visualize from the text how Isaiah, with a sneer on his face, characterizes the foolishness of the person who takes a piece of wood and with one portion makes a fire to warm himself, with another portion, a fire to cook his food, and with the remainder, a god. Then he falls down and worships the piece of wood saying, "Deliver me, for thou art my god!" (Isa. 44:17). Isaiah makes a mockery of anything that would ever pretend to be divine. He tells the people to look at the idol they worship. It has no eyes and cannot see, it has no mind and cannot understand, it has no ears and cannot hear. He declares that anyone who would bow down and worship a god of his or her own making feeds on ashes; a deluded mind has led that person astray (44:20).

We may not worship the ancient Greek or Roman gods by name, but we do give priority to the very things these ancient gods represented. The names have changed, but the object and the nature of our devotion and worship remain the same. Mercury was the Roman god of commerce and business. He ruled in the marketplace and the business centers of the ancient world. Today, we might compare Wall Street to Mercury's citadel and every brokerage house to a local chapel—where devoted worshipers come daily to sit in reverence and awe as they watch the stock prices rise and fall before their eyes on the electronic screen. The brokers act as the priests as they take their offerings and promise to turn it all into profit and fortune.

On Black Monday, October 19, 1987, when the Dow plunged 508 points, the broker-priest sought to give consolation and hope to dedicated followers that the Dow would rise again. Devotion to the stock market is so intense that on Black Monday, at the request of the Pacific Stock Exchange, a suicide watch was placed on the Golden Gate Bridge in San Francisco. During the same week in Miami, a long-time speculator who lost large sums in the market's crash walked into the local Merrill Lynch brokerage office and requested to see his broker and the office manager. He opened his briefcase, took out a handgun, and shot and killed the two men and himself. A friend commented, "His entire life was devoted to the market, and it collapsed around him." The god that he trusted had let him down.

Look at Hercules, the god of strength who ruled over

the arena and the Olympic games. Today his followers are as numerous and dedicated as ever. He has his three festivals of celebration: basketball in the spring, baseball in the summer, and football in the fall, climaxing with its greatest day of worship and devotion—Super Bowl Sunday. Millions give far more attention and loyalty to a sports team than they ever would consider giving to their church or synagogue.

The entire pantheon of the gods—the gods of entertainment, wealth, power and war, sensuous love—are all very much present and doing well in the twentieth century. We worship them all.

The second commandment tells us, Be careful! Once you have formed a visible image of your god you may be stuck with it. As time goes on it becomes more sacrosanct, untouchable, revered, and honored. The world changes, perceptions grow, new visions emerge, new discoveries are made, but the fixed idol of a static theology can no longer accommodate them. Beware whenever an idea, a statement of theology, a particular liturgy, a form of church government, a church building, or a way of doing things becomes an end in itself. Then life becomes static, stationary, immoveable, and idolatrous.

For centuries we have tried to bring the transcendent down on our level. Rather than rejoicing that we are made in God's image as we are told in Genesis 1:26, we have tried to make God in our image. We have tried to wrap God in a neat package of logical and rational reasoning—where there are no surprises, where God is controlled and God's actions predictable. In other words, we have tried to "preserve" God in our theological formulas and ecclesiastical institutions. We have tried to make God less offensive and more accommodating to our culture and life-styles. The Christ of the manger and the stained glass window is easier to take than an all-invading

Christ, a life-revolutionizing Christ, who challenges our basic axioms. But the fact is: Christ breaks through all our formulas and notions about him. The dynamics of Christ's presence cannot be defined. There remains always that indefinability of God.

All human concepts, even biblical concepts, are finite, limiting, and found wanting. God will forever remain far more than the sum total of all our human thoughts and expressions. "God does not die on the day when we cease to believe in a personal deity," wrote Dag Hammarskjöld, "but we die on the day when our lives cease to be illumined by the steady radiance, renewed daily, of a wonder, the source of which is beyond all reason."

THE SUFFERING CAUSED BY IDOLATRY

A second consideration comes from the Apostle Paul in Romans 1. J. Christiaan Beker points out in *Suffering and Hope* that idolatry is a major source of human suffering. Paul suggests that suffering in the world at the hands of human injustice can be reduced to an ultimate source, that of idolatry. In Romans 1:18-32, Paul argues that idolatry, by affecting the total domain of human relationships, brings about the awful suffering of injustice. It affects the whole range of interpersonal, social, and ecological worlds.

Paul points out that suffering in our world is not the result of God's wrath but of human injustice caused by idolatry. When human ideologies, illusions, ignorance, and pretensions become absolute, controlling factors in human life rather than God, the results produce suffering. This is illustrated vividly by two ideologies of our time: the Third Reich's Nazism and South Africa's apartheid. These ideologies have been given supreme devotion by their followers and consequently have become the most destructive sources of suffering in human life in this century. Donald Woods in *Biko*, reminds us, "The obscene laws which constitute apartheid are not crazed edicts issued by a dictator, nor the whims of a megalomanic monster, nor the one-man decisions of a fanatical ideologue. They are the result of polite caucus discussions by hundreds of delegates in sober suits, after full debate in party congresses. They are passed after three solemn readings in a parliament which opens every day's proceedings with a prayer to Jesus Christ." It is difficult for us to imagine that assemblies in the name of Christ can produce ideologies that are idolatrous, resulting in massive human suffering.

Idols give sanctions to our worst instincts. Once Aaron had provided the people with the golden bull, there followed gluttony, rioting, and licentiousness—a far cry from what happened on the mountaintop with Moses and God. It has always been so. People created Molech out of the darkness of their own being and then he demanded the sacrifice of their own children. The gods of our creation become the source of our suffering. It is impossible for individuals to rise any higher than the object of their devotion. Paul writes in Romans 1:22-25:

> *Claiming to be wise, they became fools, and exchanged the glory of the immortal God for images resembling mortal man or birds or animals or reptiles. Therefore God gave them up in the lust of their hearts to impurity, to the dishonoring of their bodies among themselves, because they exchanged the truth about God for a lie and worshiped and served the creature rather than the Creator, who is blessed forever! Amen.*

Paul goes on to say that once people's relationship with God is perverted, then their relationship with the rest of the created order becomes chaotic. He declares in the following verses that a breakdown in relationship with God precipitates a breakdown in relationships with others and with the social order and a disintegration of ethical and moral judgments, the consequence of which is suffering. He declares that, "God gave them up to a base mind and to improper conduct," and then in verses 29 through 31 he lists the pain and suffering that idolatry has produced in human life.

Although Paul does not mention it here, idolatry also brings severe consequences to our environment. Once humankind ceases to be God's guardian of the created order, creation then becomes the object of human greed and technological manipulation. This attitude results in land that is untillable, water that is undrinkable, air that is unbreathable, and cities that are uninhabitable, all of which contribute to yet more human suffering.

Idolatries are built upon falsehood, deception, and untruthfulness. They are fabrications having merely the appearance of truth. In the moment of great need they will let us down. We are constantly tempted to worship something that is less than God and in the process we each become less of a person than what God intended us to be. The second commandment is right on target. It has so much meaning—even more meaning for us than it did for Moses' day because there are so many more of us in the world today.

THE GRACE OF A GOD BEYOND IDOLATRY

A God whose face is hidden and demands that we have no other gods, such a God requires a courageous faith to obey. The very fact that we can talk about idols implies that there is a true God, who is no idol. For the Christian, this is the God of the Bible, the God who delivered a struggling people from the slavery of Egypt and the tyranny of Pharaoh, the God and Father of our Lord Jesus Christ, who continues to liberate all captive peoples.

In Christ, we see God as caring, intimate, and loving—not static, immovable, or withdrawn. The story is told by Ernest Campbell, when he was pastor of Riverside Church in New York City, of a young doctor who had no time for God or the church. It so happened that he visited a leprosarium in Africa and asked the sister who was in charge how many patients she had in the institution. "Sixty," she replied. "Your God must feel disappointment when he looks at this world of pain," the doctor answered. "But," the sister said, "God does not feel disappointment or pain." Whereupon the doctor stated, "Perhaps that is why I don't care to believe in him."

The sister had it all wrong—God does feel pain. "I have seen the affliction of my people . . . have heard their cry . . . I know their suffering" (Exod. 3:7). How different this is from the idol of wood and stone described in Isaiah 44. The prologue to the Ten Commandments, in Exodus 20:1-2, reveals how God responded to this hurt and pain. Before the first commandment of the law is given, Moses declares that the God who gave this law is the God who declared to Israel, "I am the Lord your God, who brought you out of the land of Egypt, out of the house of bondage." There was grace before the law.

What unspeakable comfort and strength is ours to know that in the midst of all our mischief, amid our scheming and bad speculations, regardless of our shaping, misshaping or reshaping of life, with all of our activities and failures, God is among us. God is not a graven image of our own longings and shortcomings. Rather God, through Christ, is among us as friend, advocate, savior, and above all as our living Lord, to correct, to forgive, to comfort, to love, and to heal.

The Third Commandment

WHAT'S IN A NAME?

You shall not take the name of the Lord your God in vain; for the Lord will not hold him guiltless who takes his name in vain (Exodus 20:7).

Whom do you trust? Whose word can you rely on? The credibility of some people is very low. In a recent survey, the credibility of politicians, oil companies, car salesmen, and some television preachers rated poorly. Their sales pitches are full of hype, and their approach is aggressive to say the least. The gas company dealer says, "I can really be friendly." The car dealer informs you that "we really listen." The fast food restaurant tries to convince us, "We do it all for you." We are overwhelmed by such attention. The car repairman meets you as soon as you arrive at the garage, and before you get out of your car he wants to know what the trouble is. Why do you laugh? Because you know it's a farce. These people do not really care for you. The truth is, when you pull up to the garage and finally get someone's attention they stick the number 732 on your windshield and park your car at the rear of the lot saying, "We'll call you when it's ready."

How many times in an election year have you carefully studied the issues? You prepared yourself as an informed voter. Honestly and conscientiously you lined up the issues and the candidates. A particular candidate was selected because you were convinced that he or she reflected your concerns, only to discover that, once in office, those campaign promises, so vital to you, were never kept. No wonder the general attitude among the public in regard to elected officials is one of distrust. Recent political scandals over the last two decades have created massive public acrimony and for some, downright contempt for public officials. The Christian church has suffered enormously from the bizarre antics of a few self-seeking television evangelists. In a recent poll, their words are considered empty, idle, careless, and insincere by a large segment of the populace. Whose word can you trust? The public feels used and abused.

What's in a name? There was a time when a good name was essential. The highest achievement was to maintain the integrity of a good name. In antiquity that was a vital question and concern because the character of a person was expressed in a name. At the time of the Ten Commandments, Israel believed that a name was filled with power and vitality. At the human level, a person's name revealed the innermost self or the identity of a person.

There was a time when the naming of a child was a significant event involving the church, community, family, minister, and friends. It was an important experience. The name selected for the child reflected both the character of the family and their aspirations and hopes for their child. A name was important. (See the section on "Naming" in The United Methodist Church's *Ritual in a New Day*, published by Abingdon Press in 1976.)

For Israel a name was so important that when a person went through an experience that changed or reoriented his or her life a new name was given. Because of dramatic

44

changes in his life Abram was changed to Abraham, Sarai to Sarah, Jacob to Israel, Simon to Peter, Saul to Paul. To know a person you needed to know his or her name. That is why the name *Yahweh* was so essential to Israel.

It is impossible to separate a person's character from his or her name. The mention of a person's name immediately conjures up in our minds certain traits of character. For instance, when we think of Abraham Lincoln, Mother Teresa, or Martin Luther King, Jr., immediately we think of magnanimity, self-giving, and sensitivity to human rights and needs. When the name of Ted Bundy or Charles Manson comes to mind, we think of the depravity of the human spirit and such words as immorality, viciousness, and perversity. A person's name has an immediate suggestiveness.

What a powerful influence a good name can have on others. Gerald Kennedy, writing in his later years, confessed in *The Parables,* "Although I left home in my teens, and my parents have now been dead for many years, there is nothing more real to me than their influence, and it will be so until I die. Some things I must do and some things I cannot do because they taught me so." His parents' name had a suggestiveness for the best and highest in life. A good name is to be protected from reckless or thoughtless use. "A good name is to be chosen rather than great riches" (Prov. 22:1).

MISUSE OF GOD'S NAME

A careless use of the holy, especially the name of the Lord, is forbidden. As we have noted, names were very important to Israel. The word *name* in this commandment refers to the self-disclosure of God. We are warned not to take in vain the self-disclosure of God's character as God

45

made the divine Self known to us. Our understanding of this commandment hinges on our knowledge of the verb that is translated "to take in vain." The most apparent translation is "to empty" or "to make empty." To use God's name in a manner that empties it of its meaning and character is to use it in vain.

The easiest way to shock another person and gain attention is by the misuse of something that is particularly holy or sacred to that person. To use the name of someone who means a great deal to a person in a disparaging or vulgar manner can inflict hurt and pain. When we speak in God's name or in the name of Jesus Christ it is to bring hope, deliverance, freedom, and healing to others. To use God's name as a means of contempt or scorn reflects the very opposite of God's intention and purpose. This would be a serious violation of the third commandment, allowing God's name to be subjected to profane and derogatory use. For some people the use of a holy name is so habitual the effect wears off almost immediately and blasphemy becomes a boring and thoughtless habit, an expression of impotence and weakness.

There is power in God's name, but this power is given for a very specific purpose such as the maintenance of the world, and for the care and well-being of all God's people. Even though we are tempted to use the power inherent in the personal name of God to do harm against others, yet under no circumstance is the name of God to be used for either personal advantage or hurt against another person.

Religion has been used as an influential tool to manipulate others—even for purposes of war. In one incident in the movie *Patton*, the general was planning an attack on a German stronghold and he needed air support, which required good weather. He commanded his officer, "Get me the chaplain!" How easily God's name can be manipulated for the conduct of war or the undertaking of any human enterprise! Far too many times, as history is our witness, Christianity has been used by unscrupulous individuals as a tool for frightening or coercing people to submit to their policies.

James Bentley, in his outstanding book *Martin Niemöller*, documents an incident I have had a difficult time comprehending. It is about Professor Gerhard Kittel of Tübingen, Germany. Kittel was a brilliant biblical scholar who had established an international reputation as editor of the *Theological Dictionary of the New Testament*, a monumental work that is still highly respected. Kittel's writings were distinguished from other New Testament scholars by their emphasis on rabbinic studies, and he went so far as to assert that every part of the ethical teachings of Jesus had its counterpart in the Old Testament.

But in 1933, Kittel defended Hitler's anti-Semitism and supported legislation against the Jews in Germany. Kittel tried to make anti-Semitism respectable in Germany. Gerhard Kittel, professor of biblical studies and Christian minister, in the name of Jesus Christ drew up the twelve articles asserting that National Socialism represented God's call to the German nation and that Adolf Hitler was its God-given leader. How massive is the damage that has been done by individuals and groups who have lifted up God's name for doing evil and wrong. The temptation for wrongdoing in God's name is ever present, even in the religious community.

This was the temptation that Jesus faced in Matthew 4, the misuse of his power and authority for personal advantage. He was in the wilderness, tired and hungry. He was tempted to turn the stones into bread. It seemed like a reasonable thing for a hungry man to do. He was tempted to use the power of God's name to obtain food for himself in a manner that other men and women could not. Next, he was tempted to jump from the roof of the temple and in God's name land safely on the ground. It certainly would help his public relations. It is the kind of thing you would expect of Evel Knievel but not Jesus of Nazareth. Then he was tempted to use the power inherent in God's name to achieve earthly rule and reign over the kingdoms of the world by force. If Jesus had yielded to this last temptation, he would have been merely one of the world's freedom fighters and long ago forgotten.

Jesus faced each of these temptations and rejected them and took upon himself the form of a servant. On that Sabbath day in Nazareth he defined his ministry by saying, "The Spirit of the Lord is upon me, . . . he has anointed me to preach good news to the poor. . . . to proclaim release to the captives . . . recovering of sight to the blind, to set at liberty those who are oppressed" (Luke 4:18).

How great is our temptation to misuse what God has given to us and to do it in his name. During the Second World War in England a woman went to her pastor to express her deep distress over the death of English women and children as a result of the bombing of the English cities by the Germans. She asked her pastor to pray that God would make it possible for the English pilots to kill German women and children. Her pastor asked her to write out her prayer and bring it to church next Sunday. She did so and after the pastor had read it he told her that she did not end the prayer as we end all prayers, "in the name of Jesus Christ, Amen." She said she could not do that, she could not pray this prayer in the name of Jesus Christ. Why? Because it is extremely difficult to invoke the name of Jesus Christ in a prayer for personal harm or death. The woman realized that the name of God has power, and that power is to bring healing, wholeness, and blessing, not pain and hurt, on others.

Helmut Thielicke tells this vivid story in *The Trouble with the Church* **that illustrates what we have been saying.**

A very well-to-do church councilman had invited me to tea in his very fine and tastefully furnished home. I expressed my regret that during the war even this gem of a house had not been spared by the bombs, leaving only a small portion of it standing . . . His reply was, "Don't talk about regret. Even in this loss I experienced the grace of God." And the first thing I thought was: How devout this man is, how humble he is—and what a superficial and sentimental way to have addressed him! Then he went on to say, "God left me with just enough room so that I did not have to take in any refugees after the war." I shall not now expatiate upon the shock which this alternating hot and cold shower of statements produced in me.

This man never understood that his relationship with God had anything to do with his neighbor's need for housing. His religious faith stood apart, separated and unconnected with the rest of his life. To say that we belong to Christ and yet lack compassion, understanding, and self-giving to the point of insensitivity to the human needs and human rights of those around us is to take the Lord's name in vain.

This commandment is a prohibition against taking a pledge or promise in God's name to do something and then breaking that promise. The statement is made, "As God is my witness you have my word." For some this means a great deal, but for others it means nothing. The breaking of a pledge taken in God's name is something the Bible looks upon with utmost seriousness. "And you shall not swear by my name falsely, and so profane the name of your God: I am the Lord" (Lev. 19:12).

There is a close relationship between the third commandment and Matthew 5:33-37.

Again you have heard that it was said to the men of old, "You shall not swear falsely, but shall perform to the Lord what you have sworn." But I say to you, Do not swear at all, either by heaven, for it is the throne of God, or by the earth, for it is his footstool, or by Jerusalem, for it is the city of the great King. And do not swear by your head, for you cannot make one hair white or black. Let what you say be simply "Yes" or "No"; anything more than this comes from evil.

Jesus is making the point that every oath is made in the presence of God. Therefore, your word is your bond—that's all that is needed, merely yes or no. God cannot possibly be kept out of any transaction by people, for God is everywhere present, whether God's name is invoked or not. God is present where any promise is given or taken. God is a witness to every transaction. All promises and pledges are made in the presence of God, and this commandment informs us that it is something that God takes seriously and so should we.

Let us keep in mind those very special moments when we gave our word before God. Do you remember what you promised? How is it with you today? Is your word your bond? Have you been honest in your vows before God? How is your credibility? Is there integrity between what you have said and how you live? Did those vows mean anything then? Do they mean anything now? The third commandment reminds us of the sacredness of every vow and promise that we have taken in God's name and in God's presence.

THE POWER OF THE HOLY

Jesus refers to God's name as "hallowed" or "holy" in his prayer in Matthew 6:9. The word for "holy" is *hagios*, which means different or separate. A name which is *hagios* is different from all other names. Jesus is saying in his prayer, Let God's name be treated differently from all other names; let God's name be given a position which is absolutely unique.

The holiness of God's name as expressed in the commandment was essential for Israel. God's name held everything together. If the people no longer had respect for the holiness of God, then there would be no reverence for anything. When God, and God's name, are honored, all life is sacred. When God is dishonored, nothing is sacred. A loss of reverence and respect for God's name causes a loss of respect and concern for one another. Rodney Dangerfield complains, "I don't get no respect." Neither does anyone else in a world where God's name is not hallowed. Jesus understood this and set the phrase "hallowed be thy name" at the very beginning of the Lord's Prayer. This is why God had Moses place this commandment near the top of the list in the Decalogue. Moses knew that respect and reverence for God's name lay at the root of all moral and spiritual value.

Today, our problem is that we do not have a sense of the holy. A man was interviewed on TV as he desperately tried to straighten the tombstone on his wife's grave. The night before, a motorcycle gang had played havoc in the cemetery, knocking over numerous tombstones and desecrating many of the gravesites. In response to the TV reporter, the man in a distraught and tearful voice asked, "Isn't anything sacred anymore?" Most people have lost touch with the concept of the sacred, the holy. We do not give much thought to the "holiness" of God's name, because we do not know about the holiness of God. In the face of such devaluation of the holiness of God we do not seem to know what is holy or sacred anymore. Nothing appears sacred, not even the name of God.

In a recent seminar, John Killinger commented on the subject of God's name as holy. He made this very poignant statement that for Israel, the name of God was the "tent-pole." It supported the whole framework. Then he went on to illustrate his point by referring to Robert E. Lee, whose name was a great name for many Americans. After the Civil War Lee became president of Washington College, which later became Washington and Lee. During his days as college president he took trips down through Virginia, North and South Carolina, Georgia, and Florida. In small towns of no more than five hundred people, thousands would come from miles around to gather at the train station hoping to get a glimpse of Lee. Mothers would hold up their little boys with notes in their hands for him to read, informing him that they were named Robert E. Lee in honor of him. Killinger pointed out that the name Robert E. Lee was a "tent-pole" when the South needed a tent-pole. The South was in despair, shame, and humiliation. Here was a man who carried himself straight and tall, of whom they were proud, giving them a sense of hope and dignity. If a human name can do so much, think what God's name can do.

The psalmist declared, "And those who know thy *name* put their trust in thee" (Psalm 9:10; italics added). This means that those who know what God is like, those who know the nature and character of God, will put their trust in God. The psalmist also said, "Some boast of chariots, and some of horses; but we boast of the *name* of the Lord our God" (Psalm 20:7; italics added).

The third commandment probes deep into our hearts. Who is there among us without sin? Who among us has been able to keep the letter of this law? If we are honest we all would confess that we have at some time misused God's name in an empty, careless, and insincere manner. But the word that comes to us in the gospel of Christ today is not condemnation but forgiveness. Paul declares, "For the law of the Spirit of life in Christ Jesus has set me free from the law of sin and death" (Rom. 8:2).

The Fourth Commandment

A BALANCED LIFE
(Part One)

Remember the sabbath day, to keep it holy (Exodus 20:8).

There is a story that Hebrew families tell their children to help them understand the fourth commandment. "The Sweetest Sound" is the story of King Ruben, and it goes something like this:

King Ruben was always asking questions. "Where is the hottest place on earth?" "Where is the place that the snow falls deepest?" One day he called his advisors together and asked them, "What is the sweetest melody of all?"

His wise men rubbed their chins and looked at each other. They opened their dictionaries and their encyclopedias. They searched and searched their books of wisdom, but they could not find the answer.

"Why not have a contest to find the sweetest melody?" they advised the king.

So the king called together all the musicians throughout his kingdom to come to the palace and play their sweetest tunes.

The story of King Ruben is paraphrased from Who Knows Ten?: Children's Tales of the Ten Commandments, *told by Molly Cone (New York: Union of American Hebrew Congregations, 1965).*

Early in the morning they gathered under the king's window. They came with flutes, harps, and violins. They came with horns, bells, and drums. They came with banjos, bugles, chimes, cymbals, gongs, triangles, lutes, lyres, and trumpets.

Their tuning and scraping and testing woke the king at sunrise. Smiling, King Ruben jumped out of his royal bed, believing that today he would discover the sweetest melody in all the world.

So they began. Throughout the morning the king sat on his balcony and listened. By noon he had listened to all the sounds imaginable that could be made by plucking, tinkling, blowing, and banging.

By afternoon, the king had heard all the melodies which could be made by whistling, jingling, shaking, sawing, buzzing, and pounding. Then the advisors asked their king, "To your ears, which melody is the sweetest?"

King Ruben listened through one ear, then he listened through the other. He listened standing up. He listened sitting down. He listened with his eyes closed. He listened with his mouth open. But the king could not tell which sound was the sweetest.

One of his advisors suggested to him that he should have all the instruments play together, at the same time. "A wonderful idea," said the king, so he had them all play at the same time.

All of the instruments blew, rang, bonged, blared, pealed, strummed, and whistled together. King Ruben wrinkled his face and listened with all of his might. The noise was so great he could not think.

Just at that moment a woman dressed in her Sabbath best pushed to the front of the crowd. It was now late on Friday afternoon. "O King, I have the answer to your question," she said. The king was surprised because she did not even have an instrument.

"Why didn't you come earlier?" the king asked.

The woman replied, "I had to wait until just before the setting of the sun."

Sure enough, the sun was setting in the west. The musicians were still puffing, blowing, chiming, and strumming. But again there was so much noise the king could hardly think. He raised his hand.

"Stop!" he said. And all the musicians put down their instruments.

Taking two candles and placing them on the balcony railing, the woman lit them with a match. Just as the sun was setting the flames of the candles flickered and glowed.

She lifted her voice and prayed, "Blessed art thou O Lord our God, King of the universe, who sanctified us by thy commandments and commanded us to kindle the Sabbath lights."

Then she took her hands away from her face. "He that has ears to hear, let him hear," she said.

The king raised his head. The advisors took their hands away from their ears. The people in the crowd stood still.

The king was whispering, "What? What is that?" He could not hear a sound.

"What you hear is the sound of rest. And isn't the peace that the Sabbath brings the sweetest melody of all?"

THE LURE OF BUSYNESS

"Being busy" has become a status symbol. There is an incessant need for most of us to keep our bodies and minds in perpetual motion. Solitude makes us feel uneasy. Most of us look for and desire movement. We prefer busyness over inactivity. When we answer the phone the caller begins, "I know you are busy, but—." We would confuse the caller and even harm our reputation if we were to say, "Oh, no, I am completely free. I don't have anything to do but to talk to you." The caller may quickly lose interest in a person who has so little to do. We love those phone calls that begin, "I know you are a busy person and I hate to bother you." Immediately that person gets our attention.

There is a need for us to fill every empty corner and to occupy every moment so as not to permit any empty space. When we are forced to sit without something to read, to listen to, a TV to watch, or a phone to answer, we become tense and restless. We welcome anything that will come along and disturb us.

Henri J.M. Nouwen confessed in *The Living Reminder* that he did not know how he would survive without books. "I keep wondering which words I can take with me in the hour when I have to survive without books." God forbid that I should ever be without books. On cable television I have access to six major league baseball teams. I enjoy a free evening watching a game. I have developed the art of watching the game and reading a book. The fact is I just cannot sit and merely watch a game. One summer I mastered the skill of watching Dwight Gooden bear down on a batter with his high inside fastball while reading *A Passion for Excellence* by Tom Peters and Nancy Austin. This is what I call my recreational reading. Also, I become annoyed by the numerous delays in traveling the streets of St. Petersburg, especially US19, along with the frequent occurrence of being held up by bridge openings. I am convinced that these boats have conspired to block my path when I can ill afford to lose a minute of time. For these kinds of emergency situations I carry books in my car. It seems so useless to sit, watch, and wait. I must admit that I have a desire to be productive, or at least give the appearance of being productive.

This summer we visited the family farm in southern New Jersey. It was good to get away from the city and to enjoy the open spaces. My son, who had just completed his spring term at college, was with us. While sitting in the farmyard under the shade of a large tree, I remarked how great it was to get away from it all and unwind. His comment was, "Dad, I didn't really want to unwind this far. To tell you the truth, if I unwind any further I'll die!" He had about all he could take of open spaces.

I notice the cyclist on his ten-speed pedaling down a country road and the lonely runner on a deserted path, each with a Walkman strapped to his arm. They also could not tolerate the silence. Our failure to have open spaces, solitude, silence, and rest throws life out of balance. There is no letup to our relentless pace. It is business as usual seven days a week, twenty-four hours a day. This commandment is saying to us, "There is more to life than this." Schedules, timetables, production charts, performance records, perpetual productivity, are not all there is to life. Don't forget the open spaces. It is here that we need to discover relationship, feeling, mutual love, and affection. We need to take time to stroke and to be stroked.

Hugh Prather talks about this in *Notes to Myself*:

> *If I had only . . .*
> *forgotten future greatness*
> *and looked at the green things and the buildings*
> *and reached out to those around me*
> *and smelled the air*
> *and ignored the forms and the self-styled obligations*
> *and heard the rain on the roof*
> *and put my arms around my wife*
> *. . . and it's not too late*

BALANCE COMES FROM BOUNDARIES

The fourth commandment shows us that nothing goes on and on without interruption. If we do not take time to slow down, then someone or something will come along and slow us down. There are built-in limits to God's design for our life, our authority, and our responsibility. The commandment deals with life in terms of concrete boundaries. Each day of creation closed with the words, "It is good." It is good that history has its boundaries. It is good that work fits within the context of rest. It is good that God's decision and design stand at the beginning and at the end.

In the fourth commandment human life is pictured within the context of an essential balance. We are creatures created for worship, reflection, sensitivity, sharing, and rest. We need an unhurried time within the balance of seven ordinary days in order to collect our thoughts and remember who we are. A life out-of-balance is like a tire out-of-balance on your car; both wear out quickly.

The fact is God has arranged time in such a way as to allow for a sacred rest. Sabbath rest is an integral part of the divinely ordained cosmic order. Men and women are not instruments or tools of labor, and work should not become the sole devotion of one's life. To disregard this balance of life, this rhythmical pattern of labor and rest is to lose an essential ingredient of our humanness. The necessity for us, as expressed in the law, is that we have a day of rest, but the day itself does not matter. This is a serious matter of personal responsibility and not, as Jesus stated in Mark 2:23-28, legal coercion.

Clearly, this commandment is not an option for living, but rather it is an indispensable aspect of creation. We have been designed to live within a rhythmical pattern. We acquire a deep sense of satisfaction and fulfillment when we cooperate with God's intended purpose for creation.

Two examples of our inclination to resist the natural order come to mind. One comes from a delightful book I recently read about a couple who wanted to spend one entire winter in northern Alaska. They were experienced campers, and they felt this would be the ultimate challenge of their life in the wild. As the winter settled in around them things were not going too well. In fact, they considered abandoning the entire project. Then one day something happened that was to have a major effect on their entire experience. During a hunting trip they were caught in a blinding snowstorm. Their immediate reaction was to fight their way back against the storm's fury to their cabin. But they realized it was impossible and suicidal to do so. They proceeded to build a lean-to against the side of a snowbank so as to gain protection from the wind and snow and wait until the storm had subsided. When the snow stopped and the clouds cleared, they safely made their way back to the cabin. This incident was a turning point in their survival. They cooperated with nature instead of fighting against it. For them to have done otherwise probably would have cost them their lives.

Our disregard for God's timetable has caused pain and discomfort. We have created a world of hostility that has led to war and destruction causing millions of refugees to roam the earth. World hunger is rampant. Then we turn to God and say, "How could you permit such things to exist?" We have misused the created order—upsetting God's ecological patterns. Indiscriminately we have used pesticides and insecticides. While stockpiling waste chemicals in the production of nuclear power we complain, "How can God allow such death and deformity of human life?" We use unlimited quantities of drugs, pills, all kinds of stimulants, uppers, downers, alcohol, tobacco, causing minds to be blown, lives wasted, and lungs destroyed. Then we complain, "I don't know how God can do this to me. It is all so unfair and cruel." The commandment points out that there is a pattern, rhythm, and balance among all things that God has made. We need to discover this balance and give it respect and reverence. To do so provides human life with both harmony and health.

The other example is our attitude toward aging. With great resistance we approach the aging process. We want to remain youthful. Some people do all in their power to maintain a youthful appearance. They abhor the possibilities of becoming old. Our tendency is to deny aging. We are unwilling to accept its reality, while at the same time spending enormous amounts of money and time on replacement parts in an effort to cover it up. There are few things as sad as a man or woman in advanced age seeking to maintain their youthfulness by using inordinate amounts of cosmetics and clothing. Their resistance to the inevitable is to fight a losing battle.

An unwillingness to accept aging as part of the rhythm of life puts one out of step with the order of things, causing friction, unhappiness, and discontent. The response is, "I don't like what is happening to me and I can't accept it." How meaningful life could be if aging is accepted for what it is—part of God's scheme of life, an aspect of creation. Here again the commandment is saying to us that we need to discover the rhythm of creation. Life is a balanced unit of time from birth through childhood, youth, middle age, and older years to death. To be in harmony with this balance of time mentally and emotionally brings wholeness to life. We must remember that in each phase of life's unit, not one moment is out of bounds of God's love and care. The words of the old hymn are reassuring:

> *Change and decay in all around I see;*
> *O Thou who changest not, abide with me.*

THE IMPORTANCE OF REMEMBERING

The fourth commandment reminds us that Sabbath rest is a time for us to remember. Our memory plays an essential role in our sense of well-being. In *The Living Reminder*, Henri J.M. Nouwen writes, "An Auschwitz that is forgotten causes a Hiroshima, and a forgotten Hiroshima can cause the destruction of our world. By cutting off our past we paralyze our future: forgetting the evil behind us we evoke the evil in front of us." Forgetting our past is like turning our most intimate teacher against us. By this commandment God has provided an opportunity for memory to function.

Remember is the first word of the commandment. If you could not remember your name, your parents, where you lived or what happened to you, you would not be you. Time would be meaningless to you. Every Jew remembers the Exodus. It is these memories, this knowledge about themselves, that makes them Jews. The Israelites were admonished to remember and never to forget: Remember you were slaves. You were the scum of the earth, merely dust under the chariot wheels of Pharaoh. Remember the times of trouble and affliction. Remember the drama of Pharaoh's brickyard! Remember God brought you from slavery to freedom, through the wilderness to Canaan, and the Sabbath will serve as a constant reminder (Deut. 5:15).

Above all remember God's steadfast love. When you were hungry, God fed you with manna in the wilderness.

61

When you were thirsty, God gave you water from the rock in a dry land. When your backs were against the wall at the Red Sea, God delivered you. When you lost your way, God led you with a pillar of fire by night and a cloud by day. When it appeared that no one cared, God cared. Remember this God is your God and you are God's people. God has decreed a special time that Israel would never forget, not only at the time of Passover but also with the rhythmical reoccurrence of the Sabbath.

The Passover is a time for the Israelite community to remember how God broke into history to liberate God's people. When we as Christians come to celebrate the Eucharist it is a time for us to remember who God is and what God has done—to remember how God in Christ came to set the captive free. The loaf and the cup are humble elements that point beyond themselves to the reality of Jesus' life, death, and resurrection. The Eucharist is a time for us to allow our memory to function and to recall the fact that "while we were yet sinners Christ died for us" (Rom. 5:8).

The Fourth Commandment

A BALANCED LIFE
(Part Two)

Remember the sabbath day, to keep it holy (Exodus 20:8).

My hometown in southern New Jersey started as a
Methodist camp meeting. In fact it was named after a
Methodist preacher, Charles Pitman. The tabernacle was
the hub of the town, and the streets went out from it like
the spokes of a wheel. Some of the most outstanding
evangelists in the late nineteenth and early twentieth
centuries preached throughout the summer and early fall.
It was the scene of fiery sermons, joyful exultations of
"amen" and "hallelujah" with the endless singing of "Just
as I Am, Without One Plea." Townspeople still talk about
the days when the trains were not permitted to travel
through town on Sunday. Passengers had to get off the
train and walk through the town to the other end and there
board another train in order to continue their journey.
Absolutely no business was conducted on Sunday.

One person described the Sunday of his childhood by
saying, "If something was enjoyable you could not do it on
Sunday." Sunday became a drab and boring imposition
rather than a blessing. In John Steinbeck's *East of Eden*,
his character Liza exemplifies such behavior. She is

described as "a tiny Irish wife, a tight hard little woman, humorless as a chicken. She had a dour Presbyterian mind and a code of morals that pinned down and beat the brains out of nearly everything that was pleasant to do." For a great many Christians the rules and regulations regarding the Jewish Sabbath were transferred to the keeping of the Lord's Day. Some found these restrictions irksome and others, helpful. Sunday was centered around church activities and it was a different day in behavior with strict regard for the abstinence of worldly or commercial activity. In rural America, the Lord's Day observances were beneficial in many respects, though it's hard for us to see or appreciate that today.

My wife lived in a small rural community on the south Jersey coast. The church was the center of activity for most of that community on Sunday. Her family's Sunday began with morning worship and then Sunday School in the afternoon followed by the youth program and the evening service. There was no thought of changing the pattern because this was the way of life. In fact, there was no other place to go or anything else to do. Of course, this was before the days of television or teenagers driving their own cars. Without any doubt, she is convinced that these early childhood years played a very positive role in her life. This was a way of life that our children know nothing about.

Because Protestantism had gained political power in numerous communities, laws were placed on the books enforcing Sunday observance. Everyone in those communities, Christian or not, was forced to observe the Lord's Day. That was the law. In Ocean Grove, a coastal community in central New Jersey, chains were placed across the streets on Saturday night and if you happened to get caught in Ocean Grove late Saturday night you could not get your car out of town until Monday morning. That law was still on the books until a few years ago.

I go back to my hometown frequently because I still have family there. In my early years we used to gather at Ballard Park, which was located in the center of town. For eighteen years it was the center of the world for me. There we discussed the most earth-shaking questions. Now when I return I discover it is not even the center of the town anymore. The shopping malls have left the center of this small town nearly deserted. The trains no longer run. They are a thing of the past. The tracks are still there, but the train station is torn down. Sunday observance as it used to be in my hometown is gone forever. It will never return. The response of most younger people is, "Thank God for that!" Many of the older members of the local United Methodist Church who remember things as they were are grieved over the loss.

With the passage of time, the nature of the Lord's Day has changed radically, but the far-reaching ramifications of the fourth commandment are ever-present. There is much more to this commandment than a mere legalism. It has something very definite to say about the way we conduct our personal, communal, and global life together.

BROADER IMPLICATIONS OF THE FOURTH COMMANDMENT

First, there are universal aspects of this commandment that affect each of us. Notice that the essential balance of the rhythmical week is God's gift to benefit not only rich people but also the slave; not only men but women; not only Jewish citizens but the sojourner and stranger. It is directed not only to the human family but to animals as well.

This commandment has strong implications for social justice. It is concerned for the servants, the working poor, insisting that they have a day of rest. This certainly ought to be a concern of every employer today. I am also aware of an apparent injustice in this commandment—that no mention is made of *wives* for the possible purpose of avoiding any suggestion that the law also be applied to domestic activities.

Also, the land is to benefit from this commandment. "For six years you shall sow your land and gather in its yield; but the seventh year you shall let it rest and lie fallow, that the poor of your people may eat; and what they leave the wild beasts may eat. You shall do likewise with your vineyard, and with your olive orchard" (Exod. 23:10-11). Even institutions are to be rhythmical as seen by the year of Jubilee in Leviticus 25. Thus, the fourth commandment makes us conscious of the interrelatedness of all creation. Each aspect has a very intricate and valuable role, and it is God's intention that creation—including men, women, strangers, animals, land, and institutions—work and function together in harmony. In this commandment human freedom is enhanced, human equality is strengthened, the cause of social justice is promoted by this legislation of divine sanction. The inalienable right of every person, irrespective of social class, is to have a day of complete rest in every seven days.

The movements of creation in Genesis are like the movements in a great symphony. Each aspect of creation has a resourcefulness and a dignity that contributes to the whole. Our failure to comprehend this indivisibility of creation produces a dissonance disrupting God's balance and rhythm of life. I believe that this was God's intended purpose in creation. Pleased with its rhythmical balance, God then observed it with satisfaction by declaring, "It is good." Finally, at the completion of the created order God declared, "It is *very* good."

But this is not what we experience today. We feel that the Bible has given us a mandate to harness, control, and subdue nature (Gen. 1:28). We have lost sight of the symmetry of creation as a harmonious balance of the natural process. Contemptuously we view ourselves as superior to nature and we are willing to use it for our slightest whims. We have leveled forests and cleared them of wild animals. The earth's irreplaceable fossil fuels and natural resources have been devoured. Our air is unbreathable and our water is undrinkable. Sections of the earth have been made totally uninhabitable. We have done it all in the name of the biblical command to "be fruitful and multiply, and fill the earth and subdue it" (Gen. 1:28). This triumphalist understanding of creation is an utterly false conjecture on our part. There is far more to creation than the mere welfare of "man." All of earth's creatures, as well as plants, have their inalienable dignity in God's sight and they ought to have it in ours as well.

Garrison Keillor, on a broadcast of *A Prairie Home Companion*, told a tale of Lake Wobegon, that as a boy he would go to his uncle's farm for the slaughter of pigs. It was an important winter event. He described it as a solemn task done in silence, the men with a grim look upon their faces as they went about their chore. One day he and his cousins wandered down to the pen where the pigs were kept. They threw stones at the pigs, taking pleasure in seeing them run and squeal. They felt it didn't make any difference since they were going to die anyway. He felt someone touch him on his shoulder. It was his uncle who grabbed his coat and pulled his face close to his, and looking him square in the eye said, "If I ever see you do this again I will whip you within an inch of your life." He turned and left. Keillor said at that moment he realized that for these men there was something sacred between a man and the animal that supplied his food.

Unbreakable ties bind all of creation. By discovering the interrelatedness of these delicate ecosystems and by respecting and revering them we then can comprehend the sweet melody of Sabbath peace. Earl F. Palmer calls this the beginning of "a shalom theology."

JESUS' TEACHING ON THE SABBATH

Second, Jesus had something important to say about this commandment. In Mark 2, Jesus and his disciples were walking through a grain field on the Sabbath. The disciples plucked a few grains from the stalk. The disciples rubbed off the husk and ate the grain. A group of Pharisees were watching them and immediately charged that they had broken the Sabbath. The disciples were accused of reaping and threshing on the Sabbath, which was strictly forbidden by the law. The accusers were dead serious. Jesus reminded the Pharisees how David and his men when fleeing for their lives came upon the shewbread in the temple. By law only the priest could eat the bread of the Presence. David ate the bread and shared it with his men. David was not condemned for what he did, because human need took precedence over temple law. Jesus was pointing out to the Pharisees that the best use for sacred bread is to feed hungry people. Then Jesus said, "The sabbath was made for man, not man for the sabbath" (Mark 2:27). Jesus points out the self-evident fact that human beings were created before the elaborate Sabbath law ever came into existence. Therefore, the Sabbath seeks to enhance human life not to encumber it with regulations. Jesus reminds us that people are far more important than systems, rituals, or regulations.

Let me do a little paraphrasing of the text. How easily we forget. The church's institutions have a way of becoming oppressive and burdensome. Too often church life is reduced to preserving out-of-date traditions and structures and keeping ancient buildings in repair. People become burdened by the demands of the church when they should be lifted up by the gospel. They are enslaved by the church when they should be set free by Christ. Certain forms of church life and practice become sacrosanct. The church, too, was made for people, not people for the church.

COMPANIONSHIP WITH GOD

Third, the fourth commandment reveals that the purpose of human life is companionship with God. Moses' charge to Pharaoh was, "Let my people go that they may worship God." This encounter with God in worship was essential, for what invokes memory creates *shabbat,* meaning rest. Attendance at worship is necessary for this companionship to take place and for memory to function. It has been said, "If absence makes the heart grow fonder then a host of people are in love with the church."

The commandment pays a rich compliment to men and women by pointing out that we are not timeless and mechanical creatures who are to grind out endless work. At times, we appear like automatons, simply self-operating robots whose main function is to produce goods and services in an endless fashion, but the central purpose for human life is companionship with God. Therein lies the genius of the fourth commandment, which seeks to maintain and enrich this companionship. This is why Jürgen Moltmann, in his *God in Creation,* calls the Sabbath "the Feast of Creation" and goes on to say, "The whole work of creation was performed *for the sake of the sabbath,*" that is, companionship with God.

In a sense our observance of the fourth commandment creates an atmosphere where our companionship with God is made possible. In *The Spirituality of Gentleness* Judith C. Lechman talks about this atmosphere in a very vivid manner.

> *I live on a mountain high above the desert. . . . The effect of temperature, moisture, and altitude upon the delicate balance of the ecosystem is dramatic and profound. With unexpected rain, the drab spring desert and summer alpine meadows turn into fields of riotous color. With a severe winter of deep snows and biting cold, the ranks of mule deer on the mountain and pronghorn antelope on the high plains thin drastically. And tomato seeds planted in the rich bottomland of the valley far below me grow to twice the height and give triple the size fruit of those planted in my yard at seven thousand feet.*
>
> *Similarly, the spiritual environment we provide causes our ability to communicate with God to flower or to become stunted. Our relationship with him depends upon our creating the atmosphere in which this communication will flourish. And creating a sound spiritual atmosphere is possible when we become teachable on increasingly deeper levels. In the physical world, a delicate balance exists that must be maintained for continued growth. In our spiritual life, we must establish a similar balance between passivity and activeness, so that we may continue to learn of God.*

The Westminster Confession of Faith asks, "What is the chief end of man? Man's chief end is to glorify God, and to enjoy Him forever." The fourth commandment seeks to make possible for us the open spaces and atmosphere that are needed to perpetuate both this "glory" and "enjoyment" forever.

The fourth commandment does not use work as an indicator of personal worth or significance. Instead it places emphasis upon the principle of wholeness. We need to hear this because we have a tendency to characterize a person's worth by what he or she does or owns. People who have meager jobs with no material wealth have few rights and little respect in our power-oriented world. But in John 14, when Jesus sought to leave a legacy for his disciples, it was never expressed in position, possessions, or power. His words were, "My peace I give to you" (John 14:27). To be in harmony with God, God's creation, all of God's creatures great and small—this is life at its zenith. It is this companionship with God that the Sabbath seeks to maintain so that we may glorify God, and enjoy God forever!

The Fifth Commandment

A PLACE OF HONOR

Honor your father and your mother, that your days may be long in the land which the Lord your God gives you (Exodus 20:12).

What constitutes the honoring of our parents? What are our obligations to our aging parents? Does God require unquestioned obedience by children? What about the care of the elderly who have no children or family? In these days of surrogate mothers, test-tube babies, and frozen sperm, the most important question may be, Who are my mother and father? This relationship of parents to children, children to parents, is the most enormously complex of all human relations, especially for those who are seeking to care for aging parents. If that is not already an important question for you, it quite possibly could be the most soul-wrenching question for you in the future.

What value does this commandment have in today's world? Parents can be oppressive to children, crushing their spirit and having a detrimental effect upon them throughout their lives. What about parents who have so misused and abused their children that they do not merit any respect or honor? A parent's desire for obedience can be tyrannical. Consequently, there are those who consider the fifth commandment as outmoded, convinced that it is harmful and should be ignored in our modern world.

Do not be too hasty in casting aside this commandment. Regardless of our desire to avoid the issues, we would be wise to recognize some basic facts about the fifth commandment. We need to remember that the Decalogue was directed first of all to the adult members of the Israelite community. The younger members were not excluded, but they certainly are not the focus of attention. The intent of this commandment was never to keep children in line and obedient to their parents. This commandment was never designed to be used by parents as a club to inflict the wrath of God on their children, coercing them to obey their will, which may be contrary to the will of God.

The fifth commandment played an important role in establishing the Israelite community. In order to have a strong community, it was necessary to have a safeguard against the misuses and disrespect of elderly parents. It was true then—it is true now—the strength of our community is linked to our care of the elderly.

At the time of the commandment's writing, elderly parents were considered to have no consequence because they were frail and aged, making no contribution. They were considered a nuisance to their active adult children who wanted to be relieved of their responsibility for their parents. It is here that the prophetic power and genius of this commandment emerges. Later, the prophets were to warn Israel that if it was to maintain a strong and stable community it must care for its weakest members: the orphan, the child, the widow, and the elderly. The reward for such a stable and caring society, concerned for human justice and the dignity of all its members, is long life (Exod. 20:12). It is a commandment with a promise.

This commandment is not conditional; it is sheer gospel. The fifth commandment changes direction. The first four commandments were vertical, dealing with our relationship with God. This commandment changes direction, emphasizing horizontal relationships with one another, as is true of the remaining five commandments. I find it interesting that the horizontal relationships of our faith are to begin with one's own family. Charity begins at home. The movement of the law in its moral implications begins with one's own parents and family. It begins at home, something that we many times overlook. It has been said that a saint's reputation too often depends upon the silence of his family.

Every generation has to find its life and freedom over against its parents, and it is still an enormously complex social difficulty. Life together in the family must be enriched by mutual care even when a member of that family is often a nuisance. The time comes when a person can no longer carry his or her load or make any contribution. Isolation at this point would be to curse that person and treat her or him with contempt. There is a solidarity here, and children must not forget that their parents cared for them when they were unable to care for themselves and that some day they, in turn, will be dependent upon the care of their own children. The sheer survival of the community is dependent upon obedience to the fifth commandment. Basic and positive aspects of this commandment are binding upon our lives today.

JESUS' TEACHING OF THE FIFTH COMMANDMENT

This commandment is binding upon us because of Jesus' example of honoring his parents. Thirty of Jesus' thirty-three years were spent at home. The lack of mention of Joseph in the gospel accounts of Jesus' adult life has led many readers to assume that Joseph died early in Jesus' life. Many of Jesus' thirty-three years may have been spent caring for his widowed mother and younger brothers and sisters. It might be assumed that he took over the business of the carpenter shop in Nazareth, maintaining the tradition of Joseph.

On several occasions Jesus quoted from this commandment. One such incident involved the use of *corban* as a subtle evasion of the fifth commandment (Mark 7:9-13). To avoid helping their elderly parents, children declared their goods as *"corban,"* that is, formally committed to God. When their aged parents asked for financial assistance, they would reply, "We cannot help you. All of our goods are dedicated to God." Jesus saw this as an insidious trick to avoid giving support to parents who were in dire need.

This incident reveals how "religion" can be used to evade moral obligations. The person who would give his money to the temple could evade his primary obligation of supporting his parents. Here Jesus utterly condemns such action. Religion should be the very essence of life rather than a substitute for it. We are tempted at times to allow our religious activities to excuse us from our responsibility to human need and welfare. How tragic that the financial prosperity of some religious institutions has been built on the misery of the oppressed, just as on this occasion the temple treasury gained from the destitution of neglected parents. Jesus' word to those of us who would practice such religious insensitivity is direct and forthright, "You have a fine way of rejecting the commandment of God, in order to keep your tradition" (Mark 7:9). Jesus was certain that any religious obligation that would prevent us from giving help where help is needed was nothing less than a contradiction of the law of God.

76

Notice that Jesus quoted this commandment to the rich young ruler in Mark 10:19 as one of the basic commandments that every person who sought goodness and life must obey. Jesus makes clear that love of God and fellow humans is not a substitute for the law; it is the fulfillment of the law.

THE MANDATE TO SUPPORT ONE ANOTHER

This commandment is binding upon us because it summons us to honor, care, and support one another. In Ephesians the Apostle Paul uses a word that is not found in the commandment—*obey*. "Children, *obey* your parents in the Lord, for this is right" (Eph. 6:1; italics added). The word *obey* develops significance when used in the larger context with the word *honor*. These two words have particular meanings in the child-parent relationship through life. The word *honor* never changes, whereas the word *obey* goes through a cycle of continuous change.

Obey is seen as total submission on the part of the child toward its parents during infancy and early childhood. Actually, the child's survival depends on this submission to the parents and their warnings about crossing streets, meeting strangers, and playing with matches.

But life's journey alters the meaning of *obey*. The period of youth and adolescence brings a strain to the earlier meaning of *obey*. In adulthood the roles may be completely reversed. Eventually it becomes necessary for the older parents to obey their adult children and follow their advice. This is a critical moment, because an elderly parent may have to give a son or daughter power of attorney over his or her estate, and there is the temptation for the adult child to misuse that privilege for selfish purposes.

Obey goes through changes during the life cycle, but *honor* never changes. *Honor,* in the biblical sense, sees life as sacred, deserving special care in infancy and as well as respect in old age.

The honor within the family is set upon a double foundation: our love and faithfulness toward each other and God's love and faithfulness as the solid rock beneath our commitment. Here we agree to both the law and the gospel, by our acknowledgment of this double foundation, that our love for each other is made possible, first of all, by God's love for us.

THE CONTINUITY OF GENERATIONS

This commandment is binding upon us because we do not live in isolation but are part of a continuity of generations. Children need their parents and parents need their children, simply because our parents link us with the past, and our children link us with the future. We need the essential dimensions these relationships provide for us in order to describe ourselves, and to understand who we are. It is important for our children and grandchildren, who are growing up, to hear those particular stories about their family's heritage and traditions that enrich their self-understanding. Children need these roots, so as to have some appreciation for the past and to discover the "rock from which they were hewn."

As parents, it is our children who cause us to have a vital concern for the future. The young couple today who has a baby has projected their concerns and obligations deep into the twenty-first century.

I am concerned about the future and what kind of world this will be ecologically, morally, politically, and economically. My children and grandchildren will be an intricate part of that world. I hope that there will be something significant that our children will obtain from their roots that will give them a sense of well-being and worth for the future. John H. Westerhoff's question in the title of his book *Will Our Children Have Faith?* seems all the more relevant.

Remember, this is a commandment with a blessing, the blessing being the very positive and good effect brought about by ethical and loving family relationships centered in honor and respect. The benefits from such propriety and decency in our living together as family and community are numerous.

LOVING AS GOD LOVES US

This commandment is binding upon us because showing respect for parents is a common Old Testament theme. By this commandment God is saying to us, Remember, persons remain persons regardless of age, regardless of what happens to them physically, mentally, or emotionally. Keeping the elderly close to the family, even when they make no contribution, or have no understanding of what is going on, is a way of maintaining respect. We need to match their activities with their mental and physical capabilities and resources.

This commandment is difficult. How can we keep it in today's world? Some of us are separated from our parents by hundreds, in some cases, thousands, of miles. Our care for the elderly is far different now than what it was for Israel. I grew up in a small town with a big house surrounded by relatives. Our house was large enough to care for my grandparents and a great aunt along with our family. When my mother put on the coffee pot, twenty relatives would show up.

Today our houses are smaller, medical cost for the elderly is expensive, and most of our families are spread all over the country. My father died within five miles of his birthplace, and my wife's father within three miles, but we are children of mobility. Many elderly parents still live back on the family homestead while their children have scattered. Now they can no longer live by themselves. Some children are very reluctant to bring an elderly parent into the same home with young children. Most of the time they don't have the space or the financial resources. But these children want to care for their parents. What are they to do? It is a whole new set of circumstances quite different from rural America a generation ago, when the extended family lived in the farmhouse—intergenerational—like it was on Walton's Mountain with John Boy and his family.

Also, our parents are reluctant to leave the homestead even when they are unable to care for themselves. Recently, we brought my wife's mother from the family farm in southern New Jersey to come and live with us. This was extremely difficult for a woman who moved into her farmhouse when she was seventeen, over sixty-five years ago. She helped clear the land by horse and chain. Her two children were born in the front bedroom and her husband died in the back bedroom. How could you ever ask a person with those kinds of roots and that kind of affection for the land and the house to leave? It was her whole life. The struggle for her children is, "In such a move are we really honoring our mother?" That is a tough, hard, and soul-wrenching question. In all reality, with her deteriorating mental condition, it was the only move to be made; there was no other choice. Now the parent had to obey the child.

Our concern for the elderly is essential, whether they are married or single, with children or without children.

Anything that would cause us to withhold honor or respect from older adults is contrary to the intention of God's command. If our younger generation should allow career, life-style, or corporate success to force the elderly to the fringes of life, this would surely be shortsighted on their part. The character of our society will be determined by our care for the elderly.

This brings us back to the word *honor.* Why do we honor our parents? Because we are loved by God and we seek to love others as God has loved us. Because our parents have loved and cared for us sacrificially when we were helpless and unable to care for ourselves. Because they are persons of significant worth, by just being our parents, even when they can no longer contribute or in some cases, communicate.

As I said, this is a difficult commandment. It touches our lives and consciences in many ways and raises many questions. Recently, I watched as my wife pushed her mother in a wheelchair down the sidewalk near our home. I could not help but think about the time when her mother pushed her down the sidewalk in a stroller. From a stroller to a wheelchair—the roles were reversed. At no time will God ever discard you or me as being useless or unimportant; neither should we do that to one another. "Help carry one another's burdens, and in this way you will obey the law of Christ" (Gal. 6:2, TEV).

The Sixth Commandment

THE VALUE OF HUMAN LIFE

You shall not commit murder (Exodus 20:13, REB).

Today, there is a massive disregard for human life. There is nothing in greater abundance than destructive power, stockpiled by the larger nations of the world, capable of destroying millions of human lives. From the Colombian cocaine dealer in Miami to the Ayatollah Khomeini, who sent tens of thousands of his young men to die in his war with Iraq, life is considered cheap and easily expendable. Some extremists among the Islam Shiites appear to have a frightening lack of appreciation for human life. On the television newscasts we've seen the masses of young men in the streets of Tehran, with blood streaming down their faces resulting from self-inflicted scalp wounds, demonstrating their willingness and desire to die for the Ayatollah. For dictators, military leaders, revolutionaries, and drug dealers, human life means absolutely nothing. With utter casualness a junkie will kill with just one thought in mind—How can I get enough money to buy more crack cocaine for another high? He or she will go to any length to satisfy the habit.

Regardless of the magnitude of the destruction and annihilation of human life around us, there is the clarion call from the sixth commandment, declaring the sanctity of human life. The word *rasah* is translated in the Revised Standard Version as "kill." But a more accurate translation of *rasah* with regard to its contextual use in the Old Testament, is "murder" (as it appears in the REB, TEV, and NIV). Therefore, there is no question that the basic intent of this commandment is that under no circumstances should a human life be taken by another person. This commandment has a direct and immediate applicability in a time when violence and death have become a way of life. The violence is of such cruelty and apparent senselessness that it defies all rationality.

Why consider such a commandment that has been so grossly ignored and disobeyed? Some may ask, What value does it have in our country, the homicide capital of the world? Pastor, you ought to go somewhere else and talk about the sacredness of life. My answer to that is, All the more reason for the proclamation of the sixth commandment. This commandment is designed to protect without qualification the life of human beings from acts of violence. Its main thrust is that life belongs to God and to God alone! What relevance this has for life in our country today! With this in mind, let us consider two important aspects of this commandment.

A RESTRAINT TO OUR ACTIONS

First, the sixth commandment has a restraining influence upon us. This restraint is what Earl Palmer calls a "holy interruption." There are many complex and ethical questions that are properly related to this commandment: suicide, abortion, euthanasia, capital punishment, and war. Although the commandment does not have a direct answer for these questions, yet it does put what Earl F. Palmer calls a "holy restraint" upon our actions and behavior. When we understand the basic implications of this commandment and the manner in which God has declared human life as sacred, then it has, if not an answer, a caution and restraining influence upon those of us who are involved in such actions.

In confronting suicide, we are facing one of the leading causes of death among teenagers. In fact, the number of suicides has reached alarming levels in all age groups in the United States. In regard to suicide, this commandment causes us to be cautious and considerate. At the same time, we must realize suicide is an act of violence by which a person takes the right of judgment, regardless of his or her competence, into his or her own hands. Suicide is often complicated by the emotional despair and physical illness of the person involved. Nevertheless, it is a vengeance against self and a violent act against the faithfulness of God, and it has a devastating effect upon the members of the family. Our Christian faith urges us to act with caution and restraint and to show nothing but loving sympathy and understanding to the person who in dire loneliness seeks this final way of escape.

This commandment urges caution in our consideration of euthanasia. According to this practice, a person who is suffering from an incurable and agonizing disease might be put to death in a kindly and humane manner, presumably with his or her consent. The Bible knows nothing about euthanasia, although it has become a controversial alternative for our modern society. This seems to be the result of two factors in today's world: one, the skyrocketing cost of medical care; two, the burden that a serious and prolonged illness has upon a family, as well as the love and concern for a terminally ill member of the family who is suffering. But the commandment urges restraint on our part to view it critically because from a biblical viewpoint it seeks solutions to the problems of life through death. Our biblical faith is a victory over death, not the embracing of death. William Barclay has pointed out in *The Ten Commandments for Today* that "there may be times when a good and a wise physician may ease a sufferer's passing from this world, but to reduce this to a matter of laws and rights and regulations would be to take a course which would be legally indefensible, practically impossible, morally wrong, and theologically unjustifiable." With careful reflection, we discover that euthanasia would lend itself to enormous abuse.

There are numerous restraints brought against us when we consider abortion. The sixth commandment is functioning well among us by warning us that abortion is never to be made easy or casual. To consider the fetus as useless body tissue to be done away with as a nuisance is contrary to the biblical view of creation and God's regard for the value and sanctity of human life. Within both the law and the gospel, the unborn has the right to be born. The destruction of any human life because it is unwanted is never a good thing and is clearly condemned by the sixth commandment. Feticide, causing the death of any unborn child, can lead to infanticide, the doing away with a deformed or retarded child or one that is intensely unwanted for whatever reason. A callousness toward life in the womb can lead to a callousness toward life in general. The sixth commandment causes abortion to be a hard, difficult, and agonizing soul-searching question. As a restraint in regard to abortion this commandment serves us well.

Capital punishment is not directly addressed by this commandment. Within the Jewish legal system it was never even suggested that this commandment opposed judicial execution; in fact, the death penalty was exhorted for many and varied crimes under Jewish law. However, because the commandment does raise the question about the sanctity of human life, it cannot but help to bring some restraint against societies, such as ours, that practice capital punishment. It seems to me that this commandment is functioning well when it causes those who condone capital punishment to consider what other options are available, and to consider what alternatives best fulfill the biblical mandate to value the dignity of human life.

The restraining factor that is suggested by the sixth commandment and deepened by Jesus' action in John 8:1-11, in regard to the woman who was accused of adultery, makes me very uneasy about the practice of capital punishment in my state of Florida. Because hostility begets hostility, from a pastoral standpoint I am concerned about the impact that capital punishment has upon the people who practice it.

JESUS' EXAMPLE

Second, Jesus shows us how to practice restraint. Jesus confronted a woman about to be executed because she had committed adultery (John 8:1-11). This crime, under Jewish law, was punishable by death. The question of capital punishment is put to Jesus by a group of Pharisees. It was a most provocative moment when the Pharisees seemed ruthless and callous as they dragged this pathetic and powerless woman into the staring light of public display. Here was the stirring interplay of the woman's helplessness, the vindictive power and judgment of the Pharisees, and the loving restraint and concern of Jesus. In this emotional confrontation, Jesus' presence creates a positive and restraining effect. Jesus put his life between the accused and the accusers.

87

Jesus slows down the entire process when he, amid an atmosphere of potential violence, calmly bends down and scratches out a few letters in the sand. The crowd becomes impatient, demanding that Jesus respond to the accusations they have brought against the woman. The accusers felt they had a strong case to execute the woman, because she violated the law of Moses. At the same time, they sought to entrap Jesus in a declaration they could use against him, so they demanded, "What do you say about her?" As the crowd shouted for his response, Jesus calmly continued to write in the sand. He wisely waited for the accusations to quiet down, because he had no intention of getting involved in a verbal shouting match. When things had settled down, Jesus raised his head, and with a level look straight into their eyes he said with quiet firmness, "Let him who is without sin among you be the first to throw a stone at her." Then he bent down once again, continuing to write in the sand. The accusers stood there in dead silence. They looked at the woman, they glanced at Jesus, then they noticed the rocks in their hands. It was an awkward moment of silence. Slowly, one by one, they dropped their rocks and withdrew.

Jesus' restraint had a penetrating effect; it reached their consciences, to the point where they focused on their sin instead of the woman's. Things had not been all that great in their own lives. How insidious their action appeared when compared with their own marital behavior. It is hard to throw the rock of accusation when one is aware of one's own shortcomings and sins. The woman and her sin became less of a concern. They all eventually slipped away, leaving the woman and Jesus alone. Jesus said to her, "Woman, where are they? Has no one condemned you? . . . go, and do not sin again" (John 8:11). Jesus did a remarkable thing by restraining the crowd from doing more harm and protecting the woman from an unjust vengeance.

The restraint of the sixth commandment, as well as the presence of Jesus, caused the crowd to stop and consider what they were doing. When all things were brought into focus: the accusers, the accused, the presence of Jesus, it then appeared to the crowd that taking this woman's life was the wrong thing to do. What influence do you have in providing a safeguard for the sanctity and respect of human life? Our jobs, vocations, actions, and attitudes can contribute to the elevation of human life and value.

Our hope today is that the force of the law, the gospel of Jesus, and the influence of our lives will exert restraint upon the actions of men and women in regard to these highly complex and moral issues. The sixth commandment is in favor of life, and life is meaningful, precious, and valuable. This "holy interruption" imposed by the commandment upon our action can have a very positive effect, alerting us to the high value that God places upon human life.

John Killinger in *To My People With Love* tells of a sermon by Henry Sloane Coffin that speaks of the sixth commandment. Killinger writes that Coffin quoted Colossians 3:17: "Whatever you do, in word or deed, do everything in the name of the Lord Jesus." Then Coffin said that what we cannot do in Jesus' name, we are not to do at all. If we cannot abort a fetus in Jesus' name, then we should not do it. If we cannot end a patient's life in Jesus' name, then we should not do it. If we cannot take our own lives in Jesus' name, then we should not do it. If we cannot build super arsenals or go to war in Jesus' name, then we should not do it. "Do everything in the name of the Lord Jesus."

If we cannot do something in Jesus' name, then we should not do it at all.

The Seventh Commandment

MAN, WOMAN, AND GOD

You shall not commit adultery (Exodus 20:14).

Early in the morning there is a knock on the study door. A distraught young businessman asks his pastor, "Can I talk to you for a minute?" He comes in and sits down, then in tearful emotion pours out from his heart the wretched tale of adultery that has been tearing his life apart. He said he had to talk to someone.

The phone rings at the counselor's office and the trembling voice on the other end says, "You don't know me, but can I come to see you?" The counselor discovers that she is a frenzied mother of a sixteen-year-old daughter who is excessively involved in sexual activity and drugs. She has come to her wits' end. The family needs help.

A young woman enters her pastor's office, slumps down into the chair, and sobs while trying to get out the story of her unwanted pregnancy. She is fearful of what her parents will do when they find out, and she does not know which way to turn. She searchingly inquires, "I have thought about an abortion, but I don't have any money. What do you think I ought to do?"

In quiet confidence a young man comes to talk to his

minister. In their discussion together the pastor is aware of the deep struggle and agony that the young man is experiencing over his own sexual identity. He is torn by conflicting sexual urges and wonders if perhaps they are latent homosexual tendencies. As the pastor listens, he comes to realize that here is a person desperately seeking the compassionate concern, understanding, and counsel of his pastor. The young man asks, "Do you think it is sinful to be gay?"

A pastor told about a middle-aged businessman whose work took him out of town and away from his family on numerous occasions. He told his pastor how he was tempted and fell into the ways of shame and dishonor. He confessed that he could go on no more; the guilt was unbearable. They went together to tell his wife the whole wretched story of his unfaithfulness. The pastor said that as the meaning of her husband's words dawned on her, she turned as pale as death and staggered against the wall. She had tears on her face as though she had been struck with a whip. He said at that moment he saw the meaning of the cross. He saw love crucified by sin.

These incidents are the causes of extreme anxiety and pain. In a time of crisis these people came to the church; they sought out a pastor or counselor. Thank God that the church, during these pressure points, is there to listen, to understand, and to show compassion. Why do they come? Because they believe God has something to say about this part of their lives as human beings; that God is concerned about the problems of human sexuality. They come because they have a desire to live by the highest and best insights of their Christian faith. The seventh commandment has something to say to us about our human sexuality today.

MEANING FOR THE ISRAELITES

What did this commandment mean to those who first
heard it? Paradoxically, no sin in Judaism was regarded
with greater horror than adultery, yet no sin was more
common. The relationship between men and women
before God was sacred. The Jews had high ideals for the
physical relationship between a husband and a wife. The
Old Testament suggests that every act of conception and
birth is the work of the spirit of God. Originally the word
adultery in the Old Testament did not mean what it means
now. The reason that adultery is singled out for special
attention in the Decalogue has to do with unfaithfulness in
a relationship of commitment. Marriage was a binding
commitment of faithfulness between two persons. It was in
principle similar to the covenant relationship itself.
Adultery was the social equivalent of the religious crime of
having other gods. Both were acts of unfaithfulness, and
both were reprehensible to the God of the covenant, whose
character was totally faithful. Adultery of one partner in
marriage involved not only unfaithfulness to the other
partner but also unfaithfulness to God. Therefore, the
theme of this law becomes one of the important analogies
employed in the Bible for describing the covenant
relationship between God and the people.

You could get the idea that the Ten Commandments
envisioned a rather permissive society. In Moses' time
polygamy was an accepted practice and this
commandment was not intended to outlaw sexual activity
between single men and women, or married men and
unmarried women. But I would caution the reader that
one needs to examine where this Hebrew tradition came
from and what it represents. It was based on the premise
that women were subservient to men; they really did not
count. In matters of sexual fidelity, only men could be

wronged. It was impossible to wrong a woman, because she had no rights: In the ancient world women were not permitted to claim or enjoy the sexual freedom that men exercised. Legally, regardless of her age, a woman was a minor, and she was not considered a responsible person. The cruelest of all was that, in general, a woman could not inherit from her father or husband, and this explains why in Scriptures, the widow is always the symbol of poverty and helplessness.

Anyone today who wants to make something out of this suggested permissiveness of the Old Testament will have to accept the idea that women do not count. One hopes this will not be tolerated in today's world.

MEANING FOR US TODAY

What does this commandment mean for us today? Increasingly our society has become more permissive. Sex is seen as a pleasurable activity that can be separated from the context of marriage. It is widely held that to indulge in lust is not at all reprehensible. There is a general consensus that it is wrong to criticize anything that anyone does. If it feels good, do it! If it is in the realm of possibility, go for it! There are those who are convinced that of all the commandments, this one must be set aside today. They stress the fact that persons have learned a new joy and fulfillment in life through the adoption of much freer relations between human beings sexually. Yet, when we take together the seventh commandment and Jesus' teaching in Matthew 5:27-30, the meaning has clarity and direction.

The seventh commandment is valuable to us because it seeks to preserve the institution of marriage. Adultery is not tolerated in the Old Testament because it threatened the stability of the family, the foundation stone of the Jewish community.

This commandment must be seen in light of the entire biblical context on human sexuality. Biblically, marriage is the great gift of God. Richard J. Foster declares in *Money, Sex and Power* that "one of the real tragedies in Christian history has been the divorce of sexuality from spirituality." He points out that sexuality is a gift to be received reverently and to be nurtured tenderly. Beginning in Genesis, the bond of marriage is defined in very high and lofty terms. Actually marriage is defined in Genesis 2:24 as a bond greater than that of a parent and child: "Therefore a man leaves his father and his mother and cleaves to his wife, and they become one flesh." Jesus refers to this Genesis passage and adds, "So they are no longer two but one. What therefore God has joined together, let no man put asunder" (Matt. 19:6).

Our Christian faith confronts the relationship between a man and a woman with an uncompromising demand for purity. The Apostle Paul in Ephesians 5:3-20 states that immorality and impurity are not even to be mentioned among Christians. Again he admonishes us to "put to death therefore what is earthly in you: fornication, impurity, passion, evil desire, and covetousness, which is idolatry" (Col. 3:5).

In the first century the Greeks believed the body was no more than the prison house of the soul, and from it came all the ills of life. The world at that time was deeply influenced by Gnosticism, which held that only the spirit is good, while all matter is incurably evil. The inevitable conclusion of Gnostic thought was that the body is evil. Thus, the ancient world had a low esteem for the human body. It really did not matter what one did with the body, it was evil anyway. It could not be defiled, since it was already defiled.

But Christianity proclaimed a new understanding of the human body. For the Christian, the body is the temple of the Holy Spirit (1 Cor. 3:16). Therefore, the Christian is to glorify God in the body (1 Cor. 6:19, 20). The body is to be presented to God "as a living sacrifice, holy and acceptable to God" (Rom. 12:1). Barclay points out that Christianity came with a view of the body that was bound to revolutionize the ethics of sex for the Hellenistic world.

If the body is designed to be the temple of the Holy Spirit, the body is good, and in all of its functions and activities it can be offered to God. Marriage, therefore, becomes a sacred and holy relationship. Paul concludes, "Let marriage be held in honor among all, and let the marriage bed be undefiled" (Heb. 13:4).

The seventh commandment adds to the biblical concept of fidelity in the relationship between a man and a woman. The biblical response to human sexuality in our ordinary life is active, creative, and positive. From a biblical perspective, men and women, whether single, married, divorced, widowed, or remarried are called to fidelity in sexual relations.

In *Money, Sex and Power*, Richard J. Foster has defined this fidelity in several directions. First, he states that fidelity means to affirm our sexuality in all its manifold complexity. We acknowledge and celebrate the fact that we are sexual beings needing tenderness, compassion, love, and friendship. We will seek to be faithful to our God-created nature as sexual beings. Second, fidelity means loyalty to our calling. Some are called to the single life. When that calling is given by God it should be confirmed by the community of faith. Others are called to marriage. They welcome their calling, providing the time and energy needed to fulfill it. Third, fidelity means directing our sexual activity into its God-given channel in the covenant of marriage, where partners say no to promiscuity before marriage and to adultery after marriage. They scorn the modern myth that sexual prowess is validated by sexual conquest.

In the Sermon on the Mount Jesus talks about the very thought of lust as being equal to the act of adultery. This is very difficult for us to comprehend. The truth that Jesus spoke is both penetrating and unpleasant. But sometimes there is nothing one can say to people that will make them like what is being said to them. This is certainly true of Jesus' words about the thoughts and acts of adultery.

His words are: "But I say to you that every one who looks at a woman lustfully has already committed adultery with her in his heart" (Matt. 5:28). Here Jesus saw beyond the externals of the law to the internal spirit where people live. Is there a possible distinction between lust and sexual fantasies? It has been suggested that all lust involves sexual fantasy, but not all sexual fantasies lead to lust. What is the difference? Lewis B. Smedes makes this distinction in *Sex for Christians*: "When the sense of excitement conceives a plan to use a person, when attraction turns to scheme, we have crossed beyond erotic excitement into spiritual adultery." Lust, then, becomes an untamed, inordinate sexual passion to possess. For some it becomes an uncontrollable sexual passion. Foster concludes, in *Money, Sex and Power*:

Lust produces bad sex, because it denies relationship. Lust turns the other person into an object, a thing, a nonperson. Jesus condemned lust because it cheapened sex, it made sex less than it was created to be. For Jesus, sex was too good, too high, too holy, to be thrown away by cheap thoughts.

Jesus is saying that intentions and attitudes are the roots from which evil behavior comes. He brings the commandment close to each of us. We tend to think of

97

religion as a checklist of do's and don't's. We get the list out and say to ourselves, "Now let's see, I haven't committed adultery. Hey! I am a pretty decent person."

It is precisely this attitude that Jesus is confronting in the Sermon on the Mount. Where one might say, "I have never committed adultery in my life," Jesus replies "Oh, but you have thought about it, haven't you? You would do it if you could. You secretly envy the person who has. So what right have you to condemn anyone?"

The world judges people by their deeds; Jesus judges people by their thoughts. The law courts deal with the end of the process, but Jesus is concerned with motive, thought, and the beginning of the process. Who among us can escape the judgment? Who among us does not need a savior?

In the seventh commandment we discover that God is deeply concerned about our human sexuality. In his book *Wishful Thinking* Frederick Buechner declares, "Contrary to Mrs. Grundy, sex is not sin. Contrary to Hugh Hefner, it's not salvation either. Like nitroglycerin, it can be used either to blow up bridges or heal hearts." The seventh commandment digs deeply into our hearts and minds. It causes us to do some serious thinking and praying. When that happens, this commandment has served us well. Richard Foster reminds us in *Money, Sex and Power*:

> *Sex is like a great river that is rich and deep and good as long as it stays within its proper channel. The moment a river overflows its banks, it becomes destructive, and the moment sex overflows its God-given banks, it too becomes destructive. Our task is to define as clearly as possible the boundaries placed upon our sexuality and to do all within our power to direct our sexual responses into that deep, rich current.*

The seventh commandment can help us define the boundaries.

The Eighth Commandment

HONESTY IN ALL THINGS

You shall not steal (Exodus 20:15).

Have you ever been a victim of theft? I know several members of our congregation whose homes have been burglarized, some on numerous occasions. One member had his car stolen four times and his house burglarized on three occasions. Several elderly women have had their handbags stolen, being knocked to the ground and injured in the process.

One young man told me that he will never forget the day when a man pointed a pistol at him and said, "Your life or your wallet!" I dare say that nearly everyone has been affected by crime in one form or another. How do you feel when you have been victimized by those who openly and flagrantly take what is rightfully and lawfully yours?

Look at theft from another angle. How many times have you purchased a product that has been misrepresented to you, or bought merchandise with the belief that it was of good quality, only to find out it was inferior? What about those times when you were deceitfully overcharged for services or victimized by fraudulent and dishonest practices? It is almost a daily

occurrence that the elderly are victims of scams. A
workman comes to their residence and promises to paint
their house or replace a roof, takes their money, and is
never seen again.

The weak and the elderly are at the mercy of the
strong. An elderly woman is no match for a strong-
armed youth in the streets of Miami. It is a feeling of
terror and helplessness to be knocked to the ground
and watch someone run away with your personal
belongings. The eighth commandment is designed to
protect the helpless. It is to keep the strong from taking
from the weak. This commandment is a necessary part
of living together. Stealing is the kind of action that, if
not checked, destroys life in community. The foundation
and stability of society depends upon this
commandment. Basically, this commandment is a direct
and general prohibition of theft. The command not to
steal simply means not to claim for one's own the
possessions of another.

THE MANDATE TO SHARE WEALTH

Beyond that, however, the commandment today also is
speaking to the opulent individual who in accumulating
personal wealth is confident that the laws will protect her
or his property at whatever cost to the poor. It has a
word to say to those who amass wealth and accumulate
goods by any and all means. The commandment
recognizes the privilege of owning property, but at the
same time warns against the inordinate desire for
property. The "right to property" and the exclusive
ownership and use of it is part of our Western culture,
and it goes without saying that this commandment has
been widely misused. In today's world, "property rights"

seem to take precedence over "human rights." People have accumulated wealth by various means, some by unjust means. Wealth brings power, a power that is used to protect the wealth taken from another person. The victims of the rich have been woefully mistreated when they dare to gain even the smallest amount of the property of the wealthy.

The Israelite community sought to prevent unequal distribution of wealth. The covenant law required the wealthy not to deal violently or unfairly with the weak. They were to remember that all Israelites were the descendants of the slaves of Egypt. They were never to forget this, because they knew the heart and feelings of the oppressed, the stranger, the poor, and the victimized. How could they then become victimizers, oppressors, and be hostile to the strangers, poor, and outcast in their midst?

The Israelite community created concrete legislation that provided for the poor and weak. This was based upon a clear understanding of God's absolute right of ownership and an individual's relative rights as steward. God, as absolute owner, placed limits on a person's ability to accumulate land and wealth. In Deuteronomy 14:28-29, a definite percentage of the grain that the land produced is designated to be given to the poor. Every seventh year, the sabbatical year, the land was to lie dormant and whatever casual or volunteer seed came up was to be given to the poor (Exod. 23:11). Every fiftieth year was to be a Jubilee year, when all debts were to be cancelled, slaves freed, and the land returned to its original owner. Even though this was never really put into effect, in principle it spoke against the unreasonable accumulation of personal wealth. The reason for this readjustment of the economy was God's succinct declaration "for the land is mine" (Lev. 25:23).

THE TEMPTATION OF "THINGS"

Palmer makes a valid point in *Old Law—New Life*:
"Once we are set free from the temptation to steal or
covet, we may then relate to other people for who they are
and not for what they own." He goes on to say that this
commandment warns against the "idolatry of
concreteness." The greedy fascination with any part of the
created order can become an overwhelming temptation to
seize the possessions of another person. We need to guard
against "things" and the desire to own them, from letting
them gain the upper hand in our lives and obscure the
more basic and essential aspects of living.

In today's world, the temptations to steal are much
greater and more numerous than in the ancient world of
the Hebrews. In the time of the Ten Commandments, a
thief was plain for all to see. Theft was simply taking the
property that belonged to someone else. Now the work of a
thief is far more subtle: the free ride on the Metrorail, an
effectively disguised figure on a tax form, the clever use of
something that belongs to an employer, or the skillful
padding of an expense account.

Each of us probably has had numerous chances this
week for theft. Our supermarkets and department stores
with open shelves make stealing far more prevalent. Today's
shrewd shoplifting techniques are almost unpreventable.

In most of our lives today we are on our honor. There is
no one looking over our shoulders. We operate on the basis
that people are honest, fair, and decent and will do "the
right thing." A good deal in one's community depends on
the honor of the people who live there. Amid all dishonesty
people do function on the level that most people are
honest; thus, we are able to maintain community. In my
college days all of our testing was done on the honor
system. The professor would come to class, give us the test

questions along with the blue books (to record the answers), and leave. We were on our own. The fact is, in most areas of our lives, we are on the honor system.

Hardly a day goes by that a person does not encounter a dishonest act. Because of dishonesty's prevalence, there is a tendency to fall in line with the rest and go with the crowd. I heard a young woman tell how she "ripped off" her employer. I told her what she did was dishonest. Her reply was, "I work hard for him and I'm entitled to it, even if he doesn't give it to me. After all, he's loaded." Even though there is a creeping dishonesty in the work place, our Christian faith requires honesty in all things.

THEFT BY DECEIT

There is a serious kind of theft that is widely regarded as shrewd. To outwit someone by adroit actions is considered skill rather than theft. Remember Willie Sutton, the safecracker, who was respected because of his skill as a thief? Folks marveled at the sensitivity of his sandpapered finger tips which could feel the movement of the tumblers as they fell into place unlocking the steel doors of huge vaults. Because he was so skillful and clever, people overlooked the fact that he was a thief. Some feel it is their right and privilege to outwit store owners and public officials. The attitude is, "It's me against them." What is gained through concealment, cleverness, or misrepresentation is theirs to keep. Those who are caught are shocked to be considered thieves.

A member of our church finance committee had a splendid idea for our annual stewardship program that would be helpful in meeting our budgetary goal. He suggested that every member be asked to give to the church the same amount reported on last year's 1040 tax form. In a church I served several years ago a man would come to the room where the collection was counted following church. He offered to take all the loose offering and make out a personal check to the church for it. We discovered later that he reported this on his tax form as a weekly gift to the church. The tax people investigated, wanting to know if this man really gave such a large sum each week to the church. When the whole matter was exposed, the man felt his only sin was in being found out. He felt he was really clever rather than wrong.

THEFT OF THE INTANGIBLE

There is theft of other than material things. Some may never be guilty of material theft but practice theft in other areas. There is the theft of time. Entering into a contract, a person promises so much time for so much money. It is therefore not very honorable to start late and finish early. The aim of some people is to do as little as possible and get as much as possible.

There is the theft of character or a good name and reputation. There are those who delight in hearing and repeating a story in a reckless manner that brings discredit to another person or casts doubts or misgivings on his or her character. Such malicious behavior can be devastating. Shakespeare wrote in *Othello*:

> *Good name in man and woman, dear my lord,*
> *Is the immediate jewel of their souls:*
> *Who steals my purse steals trash; 'tis something, nothing;*
> *'Twas mine, 'tis his and has been slave to thousands*
> *But he that filches from me my good name*
> *Robs me of that which not enriches him,*
> *And makes me poor indeed.*
>
> Act III, iii, 155-161

The most prevalent theft that we constantly face is the theft of possessions. For some people their possessions are virtually without any significance because they have been stolen and replaced so often. It is traumatic to have an item or memento that has tied one emotionally and symbolically with the past swept away by a thief. I never realized the emotional impact this could have until I experienced it.

A burglary took place at our residence recently and two special items were taken along with many other things. One was a pocket watch that had belonged to my grandfather and had been given to me by my mother years ago. My grandfather was a very special person in my life, and I cherished the watch as I had cherished our relationship. The other item was a ring my mother had given to me at the time of my graduation from seminary and my ordination as an elder. It was striking in its design—black onyx with a small gold cross in the upper right hand corner. My mother is now elderly, unable to speak, and when I would visit her she would hold my hand and look at the ring on my finger and cry. I knew what the tears meant; the ring would bring back memories to her of over thirty years ago, a significant moment in both of our lives. These two items were invaluable to me, priceless, because they linked me with my past, my family; they helped me to understand and remember who I am. To the thief they meant nothing. I was crushed and deeply hurt to have lost them. I literally cried inwardly; it was a painful experience.

There is an indescribable gut feeling to open the door to one's house and discover one's home has been burglarized. Finding one's personal belongings strewn across the floor brings an immediate surge of anger and hurt. It has been described as a feeling of being "violated." If this has ever happened to you, then you understand the intent of this commandment.

105

One of the most pitiful kinds of theft is that perpetuated on a person in need or a person in adversity. In a recent tragic airplane crash in Detroit, looters took personal belongings from the bodies of the victims. When Vietnamese boat people in the South China Sea had engine failure, Thai pirates boarded their boat, stole their belongings and raped the women. Slumlords in our cities charge the poor exorbitant rents, exhibiting no concern for their tenants, but contempt. Sadly, some of these owners are members in good standing in local churches. It's an old story of people who drive a hard bargain and charge a gross price because someone desperately needs what they have.

The poor are often victims of fraudulent business practices by unscrupulous employers who cheat them out of their wages. Others are exploited and discriminated against in hiring practices and fair hourly wages because of their gender or ethnic background.

BALANCE IN THE COMMUNITY

The eighth commandment is essential because it seeks to help the helpless, to keep the strong from victimizing the weak. No one is to take advantage of another person's need for his or her own personal profit or expediency.

God is concerned with weights and measures, scales and balances. We, also, should be concerned and careful, because justice and meticulous honesty in all things is the natural and essential expression of true religion. The Bible clearly states that there is something seriously wrong with the faith of a person who worships on Sunday and during the week is a careless and dishonest businessperson. Above all, this commandment reminds us that there is a vital relationship between faith and ethics, between what a person believes and how a person lives. We never steal anything without paying for it in one way or another. Even though stealing may go undetected by others, we pay for it in terms of our character and innocence.

This commandment is a necessary part of our living together. The foundation of society depends on it. It is part of our calling in Christ to the highest and holiest in life, as Paul tells us, "Whatever you do . . . do all to the glory of God" (1 Cor. 10:31).

The Ninth Commandment

THE WHOLE TRUTH AND NOTHING BUT THE TRUTH

You shall not bear false witness against your neighbor (Exodus 20:16).

This commandment deals with truthfulness, but truthfulness has had a rough time recently. The Iran-Contra affair revealed deceit and cover-up in high levels of government. With the help of an obliging press, the sex-and-hush-money scandals knocked the leaders from the top of religious television empires. One of the big-three U.S. automakers was caught disconnecting the odometers of used cars and selling them as new ones. In politics, religion, industry, and the stock market, recent years have been a time of deception, fraud, and duplicity. But today is probably no different than any other time except that some of the antics of public figures and institutions have become more visible.

This commandment is concerned with horizontal relationships among people, and it is deeply concerned with truthfulness of these relationships as well as speaking the truth in public. It is what Earl F. Palmer calls "the media commandment." Social communication is dependent upon the honest statement of fact. Business, law, and science have developed their own careful methods of checks and balances to ensure the reliability of facts, statistics, achievements, and discoveries. Honesty and truthfulness are crucial. This commandment seeks to protect the integrity of the witness because that integrity affects every human endeavor that depends on communication. Think of the far-reaching consequences if false scientific data were accepted as trustworthy. Our entire technological network would be thrown into chaos. All possibilities of social communication, business negotiations, scientific advancement, law, and politics depend on honest statement of fact.

THE IMPORTANCE OF TRUTHFULNESS FOR COMMUNITY

First, this commandment reminds us that community depends on truthfulness. It is directed against the serious destructive distortions of the truth that damage life in community. The cause of justice can be perverted in so many ways: by the guilty person's refusal to confess the facts and tell the truth; accusers distorting the facts; witnesses who lie; judges who refuse to render fair judgments. Two recent events in our history have deeply affected us as a nation. In one, Watergate, we as a nation experienced the loss of innocence. Our fondest dreams were shattered, our deepest loyalties tarnished, because the highest office in the land was questioned as to its trustworthiness. The tragedy of Watergate was its potential destruction of a system and a form of government designed to protect the rights of all. The minds behind Watergate sought to adjust morality to fit existing preferences. Watergate was disruptive to the cause of justice and honor in a democratic society. The ninth commandment, which seeks to maintain honest and truthful witnesses, was violated.

110

The other event was the more recent Iran-Contra hearings. Military and political leaders displayed a contempt for constitutional powers. Because they considered a certain policy worthy, these leaders felt justified in performing illegal and secret operations in order to carry it out. One key military witness admitted that he had lied to Congress, had shredded vital documents, and had falsified government reports. All was done without the slightest regard for truthfulness and without any sense of wrongdoing. The conclusion of most Americans who watched the hearings seemed to be that an American hero's crimes are incidental if done for a noble cause. Often, telling the truth seems to be abandoned for the sake of a worthy cause. However, the Apostle Paul points out in Romans 10:2 that a zeal without understanding is dangerous.

The ninth commandment is valuable today because the fabric of our society is so much a product of deception. Distrust abounds because it is generally believed that all of our public institutions are being manipulated. The commandment's basic concern is the maintenance in private and public life of justice and truth, and that it should be our concern as well.

Because no one can rule by total terror or untruthfulness, political leaders have become skillful at deceit. Helmut Thielicke has pointed out that "terror must disguise itself, otherwise it would be too frightening and would create its own opposition." How well he knows from his experience in Germany during the thirties and forties. He says in *How Modern Can Theology Be?*, "It [terror] must call on compelling ideas as camouflage. It must promise the opposite of what it really is. It must say 'freedom' where it means enslavement; it must speak of 'protecting the world' when it pursues imperialistic goals; it must praise 'humane ideals' when it is merely interested in the usefulness of manpower for the production line; it must speak of making people 'happy' when it robs life of all magic and lets a drab grayness settle over everything." If Israel was to be a viable community, truthfulness in all things was necessary. Truthfulness builds confidence, confidence builds respect, and respect builds honor. The ninth commandment is a warning against misrepresenting or stretching the truth for whatever reason.

TRUTHFULNESS OVER GAIN

Second, this commandment reminds us that truthfulness takes precedence over profit. Many times in the business, corporate, and political world, truth becomes the first casualty. Profit at any price seems to gain the upper hand, even to the point of sacrificing truthfulness. Some companies or salespersons will tell a prospective customer anything and promise the moon in order to get a signed contract or to sell their merchandise.

THE CONSEQUENCES OF DECEIT

Third, this commandment reminds us that we must face the consequences of our own failures and shortcomings. It alerts us to the dangers and entanglements that are the consequences of cover-ups. There are those who chronically blame others and seek to rig circumstances in order to shift blame from themselves. The press has used the word *Teflon* to describe public leaders who are able to avoid personal responsibility for their poor decisions. But the fact is it all started with Adam and Eve. Male egotism blamed the entire fiasco in the garden of Eden on the fickleness of womanhood. There is a story told about

Adam and his son looking in at the garden of Eden as Adam explains that they used to live there. His son says, "Why did you ever leave such a glorious place?" Adam replies, "Well, to tell you the truth, your mother ate us out of house and home." In the narrative in Genesis 2–3, Adam is quite defensive about the whole affair, saying to the Lord in essence, "It is all your fault, Lord, you are the one who brought this woman into my life. Now look what she has done! Why did you make her that kind of woman? It is a lousy world in which I have been born. None of this is my doing; I inherited this mess. Lord, if you expect me to be different you should have made the world different."

When the Lord confronted Eve and asked, "What is this that you have done?" she gave a similar reply. "It was the devil that made me do it." The desire to shift the blame and avoid the consequences of a bad decision is an ancient human ploy. But we know, as well as Adam did, that we cannot make alibis or misrepresent the facts. When we make our choices, we are responsible for our actions. At the end of the day, as the Lord comes through the garden, the Lord will not be put off by the reference to another person's sin or by our complaint about the universe. When the Lord speaks it will not be in the terms of "they" or "it" but "you." The Lord will ask, "Where are you?" (Gen. 3:9).

Behind all untruthfulness and misrepresentation is the fear of discovery. It leads to endless cover-up, and the involvement in deceit becomes deeper and deeper. How miserable life becomes when it is a constant cover-up. Life is on the decline when it is reduced to concealment and the bearing of a false witness. There is a great deal of psychological wisdom in the advice attributed to Phillips Brooks: "Keep clear of concealment, keep clear of the need of concealment. It is an awful hour when the first necessity of hiding anything comes. The whole life is different thenceforth. When there are questions to be feared and eyes to be avoided and subjects which must not be touched, then the bloom of life is gone. Put off that day as long as possible. Put it off forever if you can."

The hardest thing in the world is being honest with ourselves. Why is it that we have such an insatiable need to look so good in the eyes of others, even at the cost of truthfulness? One answer is our desire to be the center of attention. In order to enhance our own importance, we have a tendency to fabricate and embellish our stories and experiences. The Apostle Paul admonishes us, "For by the grace given to me I bid every one among you not to think of himself more highly than he ought to think, but to think with sober judgment" (Rom. 12:3). Judith C. Lechman, discussing humility in *The Spirituality of Gentleness,* writes, "We feel disgusted with ourselves as we see the number of insidious ways we fail in being humble. Clever remarks or learned quotations come back to haunt us, as we realize that we included them in our speech and writing for our own glory, not God's." How hard it is for us to move aside and to make God the center of life. Christ-centeredness brings freedom—the freedom from the incessant need to make ourselves look so good and freedom from the need to bear false witness against our neighbor.

In the movie *The Mission*, there is a very emotional and tense scene where the two priests discuss the use of violence and the taking up of arms. The remark is made, "If might is right, what place does love have in our world?" We might say, "If deception, fraud, and deceit are a way of life, what place does truthfulness have in our world?"

This command from the Decalogue seeks to protect truthfulness, a thin and tenuous thread by which all human beings are able to live close to one another and to understand one another. Jesus affirmed the words of the commandment when he said, "And you will know the truth, and the truth will make you free" (John 8:32).

The Tenth Commandment

THE LURE OF THE FORBIDDEN

You shall not covet (Exodus 20:17).

This commandment deals with inward thoughts. It presents us with a difficult task. To control our actions is one thing, but to control our feelings and emotions is another.

The meaning of *covet* is to desire something that is not one's own, to desire something that belongs to someone else. The Hebrew word *hamad*, which is translated "covet," has two meanings: to strongly seize for oneself and to strongly desire. Coveting in this sense is not altogether a bad thing. There are certain qualities of character in another person that we may desire to possess and emulate. Paul admonishes the Ephesians to "be imitators of God, as beloved children" (5:1). So we need to add something more to this definition.

COVETOUSNESS AFFECTS COMMUNITY

"To covet" is to desire that which belongs to someone else along with the willingness to use dishonest and dishonorable means to attain it. The story of Achan in

Joshua 7 is a study in covetousness. Joshua had led the Israelites in the conquest of the promised land. The taking of Jericho had been a remarkable victory. All went well with a smashing defeat of the enemy. Now the next objective was the small city of Ai. It was not as large or as well fortified as Jericho. Joshua and his men knew it would be an easy victory. In their attempted conquest of Ai they had the shock of their lives. Joshua's army was defeated and pushed back. It was a staggering setback and Joshua asked himself, "How could this possibly happen?" Then he discovered that one of his soldiers, Achan, had taken some of the spoils from Jericho—special things devoted to God—for himself. This had been sternly forbidden by God. Achan confessed to Joshua that when he saw the beautiful mantle from Shinar, the two hundred shekels of silver, the bar of gold, he said, "I coveted them, took them and hid them in my tent." He could not leave them behind. He felt this was an opportunity of a lifetime regardless of what had been said about the taking of spoils. After all, he had to look out for himself—no one else would. He was convinced that by hiding the spoils in his tent no one would ever know. But God knew! The army was defeated. Achan and his family were stoned to death in the Valley of Achor, known as the Valley of Trouble. His overwhelming covetousness brought defeat to his people and disaster to himself and to his family.

The entire story points up the fact that no one sins in isolation. How many times we have heard people remark that their wrongdoing is not going to hurt anyone else. But it does. Individual wrongdoing always has a great effect on others. Achan acted alone, by himself, in what he thought was a secret and private manner, but his wrongdoing had far-reaching consequences. It had a deep and penetrating effect upon his people and his family, as well as upon himself.

THE LURE OF THE FORBIDDEN

The Apostle Paul in Romans 7 has a very interesting comment on covetousness. To him it was the sin of sins. It was the sin that caused every other sin. The paradox of this commandment was that it caused the very sin it condemned. Paul's words are, "I should not have known what it is to covet if the law had not said, 'You shall not covet' " (Rom. 7:7). The very thing forbidden becomes the thing desired. That which I must not have becomes the very thing I need to have. To tell a child not to touch something makes that the very thing to touch. Throughout many decades proscribed or banned books frequently have become best-sellers. The prohibition not to read a book makes it *the* book to be read.

A classic example of this phenomenon is one of Augustine's boyhood experiences described in his *Confessions.* He tells of a pear tree laden with fruit located in a neighbor's vineyard. The youths in the village were sternly warned by the owner never to enter the vineyard. One night they set out to rob the pear tree and carry the forbidden fruit away. They carried armloads of pears from the vineyard not to eat but merely to throw at the pigs. Augustine says it was not the pears his soul coveted, because he had plenty at home, but he picked them simply in order to become a thief. The desire to steal was awakened in him by the prohibition against stealing. The pears became desirable simply because they were forbidden.

What both Paul and Augustine are saying is, there is the clash between the tenth commandment and desire. Both of these men found the beginning of moral life in the discovery that they wanted something that they should not have. Therefore, the law awakens our sense of sin. When the law forbids what the appetite desires, it forces us to examine seriously what we purpose to do. This commandment pushes us back to that point where we develop our motives and desires for conduct.

The fact is that we are so built, made, and constructed that we must desire something. These instinctive, insatiable desires of ours are the strongest part of our natures. They constitute the dynamic force and power within us. The executives on Madison Avenue have discovered this about human nature and constantly play upon these desires. The value of any powerful force or desire depends on the use we make of it. I recently read William Shirer's *The Nightmare Years 1930–1940,* a vivid account of Hitler's rise to power. Shirer was an eyewitness to the vast historical material about which he writes. He was present when Hitler made the earliest speeches in his rise to power. He saw this life develop into a powerful, influential force in human history. He said the tragedy of history is that this dynamic, prominent personality could have been used for good. At the time of Hitler, Göring, and Goebbels there were also Niemöller, Bonhoeffer, and Schweitzer. Desire cannot be eradicated from the human heart. Men and women will always covet something, either good or evil. When Jesus Christ reigns in the human heart, the desire for wrong is overcome and the desire for good can become a dynamic force within a life. Why were Niemöller, Bonhoeffer, and Schweitzer different from those of the Third Reich? Because they were Christ-centered men. Their energy, desires, and ambitions were directed toward the kingdom of God.

SELF-DECEPTION ENGENDERED BY COVETOUSNESS

Covetousness leads us to false assumptions—that bigger is better, more is necessary, and to possess is essential. Richard J. Foster challenges us to learn the truth that to increase the quality of life means to decrease material desire. He said we need to close our ears to ads that bellow their four-letter obscenities, "more, more, more!" We need to stress the quality of life above the quantity of life. How easy it is to be seduced into defining life in terms of having rather than being. In *The Freedom of Simplicity,* he relates:

> *I still remember the day this reality struck me with unusual force. I was passing by some very expensive homes, and began pondering our perennial tendency to want something bigger, better, and more plush. ... Was it possible, I wondered, to come to the place where you do not desire more house even if you can afford it? ... The response was swift: "Oh yes! It is not necessary to always crave more. You **can** live contented with what you have, with no further desire to accumulate more." I'm quite sure I have not attained this holy contentment, but from time to time I have known a measure of its liberating graces and have found it a wonderful resting place.*
>
> *Think of the misery that comes into our lives by our restless gnawing greed. ... And most destructive of all, our flashy cars and sports spectaculars and backyard pools have a way of crowding out much interest in civil rights or inner city poverty or the starved masses of India. Greed has a way of severing the cords of compassion.*

We do not need to be imprisoned by a relentless spirit of covetousness that creates a craving for the wealth and possessions of others. The peace and serenity as expressed in the life of the Apostle Paul is summed up by his statement "Not that I complain of want; for I have learned, in whatever state I am, to be content" (Phil. 4:11).

We need to resist the current fetish to own and possess. Ownership has become an obsession of our culture. In reality people do not "own," they merely "have" possessions. When you come right down to it, we live in houses and drive cars that are owned by finance companies and banks. In essence, the desire to own has created an enormous burden of accumulated debt. The desire for ownership, rather than liberating people, has brought bondage to many. We need to learn to enjoy things without owning them. In our communities there are many things to be enjoyed—parks, libraries, cultural activities—without feeling we have to buy a piece of them. May the Holy Spirit help us to overcome a selfish covetousness that results in greed. Paul warns Timothy that "those who desire to be rich fall into temptation, into a snare, into many senseless and hurtful desires that plunge men into ruin and destruction" (1 Tim. 6:9).

Our contemporary society is overwhelmed by a lust for affluence. In *Celebration of Discipline*, Richard J. Foster calls this lust for affluence psychotic. "It is psychotic because it has completely lost touch with reality. . . . This psychosis permeates even our mythology. The modern hero is the poor boy who becomes rich rather than the Franciscan or Buddhist ideal of the rich boy who voluntarily becomes poor. (We still find it hard to imagine that either could happen to a girl!) Covetousness we call ambition. Hoarding we call prudence. Greed we call industry."

We are so consumed with the desire to accumulate and possess that we lose sight of the more important issues in life. The story is told that Rudyard Kipling, speaking to a university graduating class, advised the graduates not to care too much for money, power, or fame. He told them that someday they would meet a person who cared for none of these things and then they would know how poor they were. In Jesus Christ we have met that person.

There is a tale about a melancholy king who had everything but still was sad and unhappy. He was told by a friend that if he could get the shirt of a perfectly happy man in his kingdom and wear it, he too would be happy. The king discovered that the happiest man in his kingdom had no shirt!

If the possession of things meant happiness and

contentment, then our age would be the happiest and most contented age in history. Jesus' words speak to us forcefully: "Take heed, and beware of all covetousness; for a man's life does not consist in the abundance of his possessions" (Luke 12:15).

Viktor Frankl, in his classic book *Man's Search for Meaning,* which consists of Frankl's memories and observations of life in a Nazi prison camp, says "As the inner life of the prisoner tended to become more intense, he also experienced the beauty of art and nature as never before." Somehow deprivation made the eye more observant, the ear more attentive. Frankl goes on to give this moving example:

> *One evening, when we were already resting on the floor of our hut, dead tired, soup bowls in hand, a fellow prisoner rushed in and asked us to run out to the assembly grounds and see the wonderful sunset. Standing outside we saw sinister clouds glowing in the west and the whole sky alive with clouds of ever-changing shapes and colors, from steel blue to blood red. The desolate grey mud huts provided a sharp contrast, while the puddles on the muddy ground reflected the glowing sky. Then, after minutes of moving silence, one prisoner said to another, "How beautiful the world could be!"*

Today we are imprisoned by our chrome-plated world fabricated by our covetousness. We have been imprisoned by our asphalt jungles, plastic cards, consumerism, artificial turf, smog, and saturation advertising. In *For God's Sake, Be Human,* John Killinger suggests that "we are the first generation in the history of [humanity] to commit suicide by orgy." Although a generation has passed since he wrote these words, we still do not realize what we are doing to ourselves. By our oppressive covetousness we have become dead to feeling and insensitive to wonder. In our artificial, chrome-plated world stands Jesus Christ who reminds us how beautiful life could be.

A CONCLUDING COMMENT

The Ten Commandments are a vital part of our contemporary world. They bring to us a sense of permanency and durability in our search for truth and identity. The Decalogue reveals God's purpose, promise, and design for our daily lives as well as our life together in global terms.

The Decalogue is at the heart of the Old Testament message. It is part of the root system from which that message comes. A clearer understanding of the Torah seems essential for an understanding of the love and grace of God. These ten words are of vital importance to contemporary Christians, absolutely binding on the human conscience for the following reasons.

1. *The Ten Commandments reveal a God who cares.* **No study of the commandments is complete without serious consideration of the God who spoke the commandments into existence. The prologue to the law (Exod. 20:2) reminds us that grace (God's love in action) preceded the law. From the beginning of the Exodus narrative the emphasis is on grace. God's gracious act in delivering the Israelites from slavery sets the tone for the giving of the commandments. God's grace is still primary in our lives.**

123

First, we are saved by grace, the unmerited goodness of God, before we take on the obligations of law. It is God's grace that sets the captive free, not the law. Second, we then assume the responsibility of the law in grateful thanksgiving for grace.

2. *The Ten Commandments are a statement of the will of God for all times.* Jesus affirms this durability of the law when he declared, "For truly, I say to you, till heaven and earth pass away, not an iota, not a dot, will pass from the law until all is accomplished" (Matt. 5:18). It is interesting to note that the *iota* is the smallest of the Greek letters and the *dot* is but a stroke of a letter or a part of a letter.

The Torah helps us discover God's grand design and our place within it.

3. *There is the need for law.* If we are going to live together we must agree on certain laws and stick to them. This is essential for human survival. Modern human life would be unthinkable without externally defined boundaries and internal disciplines.

Can you imagine playing a college football game without rules or referees to enforce them? It would be bedlam on the field. The carnage on our highways would be horrendous if all the traffic laws were suspended and all the highway patrol officers recalled. Without civil and criminal laws enforced promptly and fairly, the community's power to protect human life would collapse. Life without law is unthinkable.

The people of Israel had been slaves for over four hundred years in Egypt. As soon as they were freed by Moses, they were on their own for the first time in centuries. The very first thing they needed was a set of laws by which they might live and become not a rabble but a real community. This is exactly what they got in the Ten

Commandments. The commandments were the rules of life. They were not only the basis for Israel's life, but they are the basis for any group of people who seek to live together. That is why they are irreplaceable for us today. This leads us to our next point.

4. *The Ten Commandments were first given to a community.* Unlike later legislation in the Old Testament that was given to Moses alone, the Ten Commandments were given to the entire nation standing at respectful attention at the foot of the mountain with the sight of God's smoke and the sound of God's thunder before them.

Possibly the most significant aspect of the Ten Commandments is the practical value of the law in regard to our corporate and social life together. One of the Decalogue's primary functions is to provide the adhesiveness necessary to form the community of all God's people. For any people who are seeking to live together, the Ten Commandments are essential.

5. *The Ten Commandments get us back to the biblical view of human nature and corporate living.* Today there is a driving desire for personal success without any thought of self-discipline or social responsibility. People yearn for meaning in their lives, but they want it without serious social involvement.

Discipline and responsibility are not fashionable today. The word *authority* is threatening to those who are hung up on doing their own thing. It is at this point that the commandments bring us to an awareness that we are to be socially responsible people living in a world deeply tied together by social interaction. Our definitions of fulfillment must depend on our neighbor's fulfillment.

No society can survive long without its own working version of the Ten Commandments. We need the restraints, guidance, grace, and authority (if you please) of the Ten Commandments if we are to live responsibly in any political society.

The Ten Commandments remind us of God's expectations for human life together. They set minimal standards for any person or group of people who dare to confess the name of Jesus Christ.

6. *The Ten Commandments had a remarkable relevance for Moses and his people, and they have an enduring significance and meaning for our modern world.* In the human drama through the years the characters change, but human relationships, values, fears, frustrations, and anxieties remain the same. It is at this point of contemporary relevance that the Ten Commandments play such an important role in modern life.

The unreasoned and unrestricted doing of what comes naturally in any generation leads to personal disorientation and disorder. God gave the Israelites the commandments in order to rescue them from self-destruction. Likewise, the commandments are available for our generation because of God's respect for human freedom and God's demand that we be morally responsible social beings.

The Ten Commandments are essential in our effort to build a humane world. Without God's moral direction in our lives, we are merely erecting our proud towers of massive technology that lead nowhere.

Finally, the weakness of the law is its inability to heal the brokenness that it discovers. The law functions in our lives in a significant manner and role that only it can do. The law is the schoolmaster or custodian (*paidagogos*) that brings us to Christ. But we need more than the law. The law points to our need for a Savior, but it is not the Savior. The Apostle Paul says it best:

A Concluding Comment

For God has done what the law, weakened by the flesh, could not do: sending his own Son in the likeness of sinful flesh and for sin, he condemned sin in the flesh, in order that the just requirement of the law might be fulfilled in us, who walk not according to the flesh but according to the Spirit.   *Romans 8:3-4*

STUDY QUESTIONS
For Further Consideration and Discussion

INTRODUCTION

☐ 1. What are the practical values of the Ten Commandments for our modern world?

☐ 2. Why is it necessary to establish the fact of God's grace prior to the law? What is the significance of the prologue in Exodus 20:1-2 and Deuteronomy 5:6?

☐ 3. Consider for discussion: The ten words (the Decalogue) given by God remain constant throughout history, while the body of legislation given by Moses changes from time to time.

☐ 4. Define the *Torah*.

☐ 5. When were the Ten Commandments probably written down? Why is this date significant?

☐ 6. The law was essential in organizing and establishing Israel as a community. What role do the Ten Commandments play in establishing and maintaining community today?

☐ 7. Read Matthew 5:17-20. What is Jesus' relationship to the law? Explain Paul's views in Romans 10:4 and Galatians 3:24.

☐ 8. How can we make good use of the Decalogue in both our liturgy and confirmation classes today?

THE FIRST COMMANDMENT

☐ 1. Comment on Walter Harrelson's statement in *The Ten Commandments and Human Rights* that "the first commandment is a summary of the entire Ten Commandments and it is the foundation of biblical religion as a whole."

☐ 2. This commandment is expressed negatively. What are its positive implications?

☐ 3. The Hebrews found in Canaan that religion and agriculture were closely related. Their greatest temptation came from the gods of fertility. Today, there is a close relationship between religion and nationalism. What temptations does this present to Christians today in regard to the first commandment?

☐ 4. What is the relationship between the first commandment and the *Shema* in Deuteronomy 6:4-9?

☐ 5. Discuss the movement of belief about God from polytheism (the belief in more than one god or in many gods) to monotheism (the doctrine or belief that there is only one God).

☐ 6. How does the character of the god that is worshiped affect human behavior?

☐ 7. What is the relationship between faith and ethics, belief and personal conduct?

☐ 8. What is the relationship between this commandment and the words of Jesus in Matthew 22:36-40?

☐ 9. Is there a connection between the prologue, Exodus 20:1-2, and the first commandment?

THE SECOND COMMANDMENT

☐ 1. Consider John Calvin's statement that Israel is to make no image of God, but Israel is to be such an image of God in the world.

☐ 2. What does the commandment mean when it characterizes God as a jealous God?

☐ 3. How is it that humans fall captive to graven images? What is there about human nature that makes us project onto particular objects and powers a meaning that these objects and powers do not have?

☐ 4. Comment on the statement: Whenever things become more important to us than persons, then idolatry has entered into our lives.

☐ 5. What are the modern forms of idolatry?

☐ 6. How can patriotism and nationalism contribute to idolatry?

THE THIRD COMMANDMENT

☐ 1. What do you think it means to take the name of the Lord in vain? What is the significance of the Hebrew meaning of the word *vain*, which is actually interpreted "to make empty"?

☐ 2. Comment on the statement: Profanity, in the simple sense, is considered as too narrow a subject for this commandment in its original setting. What are the broader aspects of this commandment?

☐ 3. How is the power inherent in the name of God used for good? How can it be misused?

☐ 4. What is the significance of Jesus' words "Hallowed be thy name" (Matthew 6:8) in relation to this commandment?

☐ 5. What meaning do Jesus' words in Matthew 5:33-37 add to this commandment? Is it important to keep your vows? Is your word your bond?

☐ 6. Discuss the significance of the punishment for violating this commandment: "for the Lord will not hold him guiltless who takes his name in vain."

THE FOURTH COMMANDMENT
(Part One)

☐ 1. What is the meaning of this intrinsic rhythm of work and rest for our lives today? Are you rhythmic in your own week? If not, what parts are out of balance?

☐ 2. What is the difference between the Sabbath for the Jew and the Lord's Day for the Christian? Does the Sabbath have any meaning for the Christian?

☐ 3. Do the sabbatical and the jubilee years have any meaning for our modern world?

☐ 4. During his public ministry, Jesus confronted more confusion and antagonism concerning the fourth commandment than all the rest of the law. Why?

☐ 5. Of all the commandments, this one would appear to have little or no meaning for men and women today—especially from the standpoint of human behavior. How do you account for this?

THE FOURTH COMMANDMENT
(Part Two)

☐ 1. Discuss the point that this commandment contains a dual obligation—to work *six* days and to rest *one* day.

☐ 2. The reasons for observing the Sabbath in Exodus 20:11 and Deuteronomy 5:15 are different. What is the significance of these two reasons?

☐ 3. Discuss the significance of the statement that this commandment is not an option for living but rather an indispensable aspect of creation.

☐ 4. The very first word of the commandment admonishes us to *remember*. What role does memory have to play in this commandment?

☐ 5. What is the meaning of Jesus' words in Mark 2:27 in regard to this commandment?

THE FIFTH COMMANDMENT

☐ **1.** In what way does the horizontal movement of the law's ethical implications begin with our own parents?

☐ **2.** Is it accurate to say that this commandment is directed to the adult children of the community as they relate to their older parents, rather than to parent–children relationships?

☐ **3.** Does Deuteronomy 21:18-21 relate to this commandment? Does this seem to be outmoded and pernicious for contemporary life?

☐ **4.** Comment on the statement: Keeping elderly parents close to the other members of the family is one of the most effective ways of engendering real respect for parents and is a safeguard against treating the elderly with contempt. How can this be done today with our older parents?

☐ **5.** Comment on the statement: This commandment is not conditional; it is sheer gospel.

☐ **6.** This is a commandment with a promise. What are the benefits resulting from having honor and respect for the elderly? Does care for the elderly affect the character of a community?

☐ **7.** Comment on the statement: As parents and children age, their roles are reversed. Why is this necessary? What place does honor play in this role change?

☐ **8.** In Matthew 15:4-6 Jesus comments on the subtle ways children seek to avoid helping their elderly parents. How is this being done by children today?

☐ 9. What value does this commandment have in today's world where parents are oppressive and abusive to their children? Do all parents warrant honor and respect?

THE SIXTH COMMANDMENT

☐ 1. If human life belongs to God and is sacred, then how is a community justified in the taking of human life?

☐ 2. Did Israel distinguish between murder and judicial killing? What significance does this distinction make?

☐ 3. What is your response to the comment: If God commands that an act of warfare be engaged in, then the people need feel no compunction in carrying out that kind of action, even though it may result in the death of many. What if a nation gives the same command?

☐ 4. Do you believe that just wars do not exist and probably never did exist?

☐ 5. How can we work to protect the sacredness of human life today?

☐ 6. What bearing do Jesus' words and actions in Matthew 5:21-22 and John 8:1-11 have upon this commandment?

THE SEVENTH COMMANDMENT

☐ 1. Why was this commandment important for the Hebrew community? What positive role did it perform?

☐ 2. Does this commandment have any relevance in our modern Christian community?

☐ 3. Respond to the comment: So long as physical harm to the sexual partner is avoided and so long as no party is exploited by the other, persons can and should find sexual enjoyment in whatever way works for them.

☐ 4. Discuss the statement: Adultery breaks a commitment that has been made between two people and destroys a relationship, the family.

☐ 5. In Matthew 5:27-28 Jesus talks about the very thoughts of lust as being equal to the acts of adultery. Is this statement realistic? Is there any distinction between "lust" and "fantasy"?

☐ 6. What boundaries does this commandment place upon our understanding of human sexuality?

THE EIGHTH COMMANDMENT

☐ 1. What positive role did this commandment play in establishing the Hebrew community? What role does it play in developing community today?

☐ 2. What does this commandment say to the wealthy individual who in accumulating personal wealth is confident that the laws will protect his or her property at whatever costs to the poor?

☐ 3. What is the function of this commandment in today's world where "property rights" seem to take precedence over "human rights"?

☐ 4. How is the potential for theft increased in our modern, technological society?

☐ 5. Comment on the statement: This law dictates that we not take advantage of another person's need for the purpose of our own profit or gain. What are examples of this kind of exploitation today?

☐ 6. What are your greatest temptations or opportunities for theft? How are you able to overcome such temptations?

THE NINTH COMMANDMENT

☐ 1. Why does community life together depend on public truthfulness?

☐ 2. Why is it that in our business, corporate, and political worlds truth becomes the first casualty?

☐ 3. Why is there a lack of public trust today? Why do people feel deceived by politicians, corporations, and public institutions?

☐ 4. Comment on the statement: Public morality is often said to be a matter of concern only to the middle-class, of no interest to the extreme upper-class, and a luxury that the poor cannot afford.

☐ 5. Comment on the statement: A God of faithfulness, who does not deal deceitfully with his people, required of his people the same transparency and honesty in personal relationships. What is the significance of such a statement for our lives?

☐ 6. The direct result of untruthfulness and misrepresentation is the fear of discovery and endless "cover-up." What effect does this have on personal and corporate life today?

THE TENTH COMMANDMENT

☐ 1. Define the word *covetousness*.

☐ 2. Does this commandment mean that a person's desire for goods or possessions like those of a neighbor is wrong?

☐ 3. What are the basic implications of this commandment for us today?

☐ 4. Do you agree that this commandment is a summary of the previous nine and that it forms a subtle conclusion for the Decalogue?

☐ 5. In Matthew 5:21-48 is it true that Jesus dealt with the thought rather than the deed? Is this idea of any importance to us?

☐ 6. What is the meaning of Paul's statement "I should not have known what it is to covet if the law had not said, 'You shall not covet' " (Rom. 7:7)?

SUGGESTED READING FOR FURTHER STUDY

Anderson, Bernhard W. *Understanding the Old Testament.* Englewood Cliffs, NJ: Prentice-Hall, 1975.

Barclay, William. *The Ten Commandments for Today.* New York: Harper & Row, 1973.

Brueggemann, Walter. *The Creative Word: Canon as a Model for Biblical Education.* Philadelphia: Fortress Press, 1982.

——————. *Genesis:* Interpretation Bible Commentary. Atlanta: John Knox Press, 1982.

——————. *Hope within History.* Atlanta: John Knox Press, 1986.

——————. *The Land.* Philadelphia: Fortress Press, 1977.

——————. *Living Toward a Vision: Biblical Reflections on Shalom.* New York: United Church Press, 1984.

Calvin, John. *Sermons on the Ten Commandments.* Edited and translated by Benjamin Farley. Grand Rapids, MI: Baker Book House, 1980.

Childs, Brevard S. *The Book of Exodus: A Critical, Theological Commentary.* Philadelphia: Westminster Press, 1974.

Craigie, Peter C. *The Book of Deuteronomy:* The New International Commentary on the Old Testament. Grand Rapids, MI: William B. Eerdmans, 1976.

Davidson, Joy. *Smoke on the Mountain: An Interpretation of the Ten Commandments.* Philadelphia: Westminster Press, 1954.

Finegan, Jack. *Let My People Go.* New York: Harper & Row, 1963.

Harrelson, Walter. *The Ten Commandments and Human Rights.* Philadelphia: Fortress Press, 1980.

Killinger, John. *To My People with Love: The Ten Commandments for Today.* Nashville: Abingdon, 1989.

Miller, D. Patrick, Jr. "The Place of the Decalogue in the Old Testament and Its Law." *Interpretation: A Journal of Bible and Theology.* (July, 1989): 229-242.

Palmer, Earl F. *Old Law—New Life: The Ten Commandments and New Testament Faith.* Nashville: Abingdon, 1984.

Seamands, David A. *God's Blueprint for Living: New Perspectives on the Ten Commandments.* Wilmore, KY: Bristol Books, 1988.

ABOUT THE AUTHOR

John A. Stroman, a United Methodist pastor, is senior
minister of Pasadena Community Church in St. Petersburg, Florida. He has served other congregations in the
Florida Conference as well as congregations in the Southern New Jersey Conference. He holds the B.A. from Taylor
University, the M.Div. from Crozer Theological Seminary,
and the Th.D. from Boston University School of Theology.
He received the John P. Crozer Fellowship to attend
Boston University for his doctoral studies, where he
focused on church history with special emphasis on American church history.